KU-499-098

CONTENTS

INTRODUCTION

The man and his myth. The problem when dealing with German generals of World War II is distinguishing between myth and reality. This is particularly difficult given that their histories and characters are constantly being re-examined. The myth of Erwin Rommel – the 'Desert Fox' – has proved to be particularly long lasting. There are many historical issues surrounding his true merits as a military commander and the extent of his actual involvement in the anti-Hitler conspiracy, and yet on close inspection he comes across as a simple, straightforward man whose talents and character ensured his success in the very particular circumstances that arose throughout his career.

Rommel's family background provides few clues to his future military success. He was born far away from militarist Prussia; in the Austro-Prussian war of 1866 Württemberg, his homeland, was an Austrian ally and as such was defeated, eventually becoming part of the new German Empire (though still retaining its own army as an independent entity in the new German Army). His family had no military background, and he himself displayed no interest at all in a career in the army during his boyhood. His only known childhood enthusiasm was for aeronautical engineering and a desire to work for the renowned Zeppelin works.

Erwin Rommel, the 'Desert Fox' in a typical portrait. Other than the captured British sand goggles, he sports the Pour le Mérite and the Knight's Cross with oak leaves, which were awarded on 20 March 1941. (HITM)

As a cadet Rommel was workmanlike rather than impressive, and it would take the first battlefield tests to reveal how Rommel's talent and character, supported by a solid military education, had produced a brave and effective commander.

Rommel's performance in World War I earned him a position in the small post-war army of the Weimar Republic, the Reichswehr. Again, he neither excelled nor failed and would have most probably ended his career as a divisional or, at best, corps commander had it not been for his close relationship with Hitler. Thanks to this relationship he was given command of one of the ten

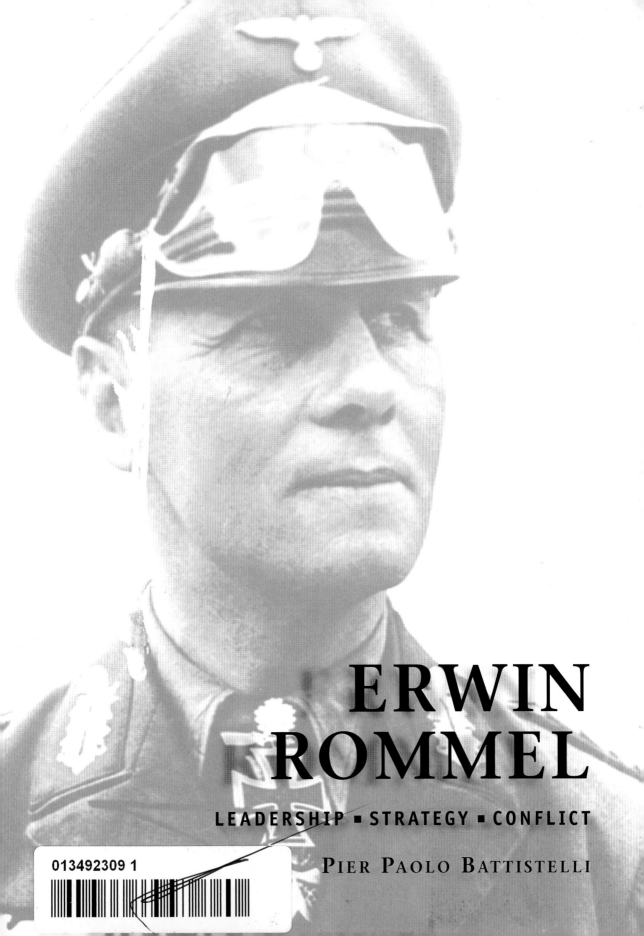

ERWIN
ROMMEL

LEADERSHIP ■ STRATEGY ■ CONFLICT

PIER PAOLO BATTISTELLI

First published in Great Britain in 2010 by Osprey Publishing,
Midland House, West Way, Botley, Oxford OX2 0PH, UK
44-02 23rd St, Suite 219, Long Island City, NY 11101, USA

E-mail: info@ospreypublishing.com

© 2010 Osprey Publishing Ltd

A CIP catalogue record for this book is available from the British Library.

ISBN: 978 1 84603 685 9
E-book ISBN: 978 1 849082 88 4

Editorial by Ilios Publishing Ltd, Oxford, UK (www.iliospublishing.com)
Page layout by Myriam Bell Design, France
Index by Michael Forder
Typeset in Stone Serif and Officina Sans
Maps by Mapping Specialists Ltd
Originated by PDQ Media, Bungay, UK
Printed in China through Worldprint Ltd

10 11 12 13 14   10 9 8 7 6 5 4 3 2 1

FOR A CATALOGUE OF ALL BOOKS PUBLISHED BY OSPREY
MILITARY AND AVIATION PLEASE CONTACT:

Osprey Direct, c/o Random House Distribution Center,
400 Hahn Road, Westminster, MD 21157
Email: uscustomerservice@ospreypublishing.com

Osprey Direct, The Book Service Ltd, Distribution Centre,
Colchester Road, Frating Green, Colchester, Essex, CO7 7DW
E-mail: customerservice@ospreypublishing.com

www.ospreypublishing.com

The Woodland Trust
Osprey Publishing are supporting the Woodland Trust,
the UK's leading woodland conservation charity, by funding
the dedication of trees.

Artist's note

Readers may care to note that the original paintings from which the
colour plates in this book were prepared are available for private sale. The
Publishers retain all reproduction copyright whatsoever. All enquiries
should be addressed to:

Peter Dennis, Fieldhead, The Park, Mansfield, Notts, NG18 2AT, UK

The Publishers regret that they can enter into no correspondence upon
this matter.

Table of ranks

German	British	USA
Leutnant	Second Lieutenant	Second Lieutenant
Oberleutnant	Lieutenant	First Lieutenant
Hauptmann	Captain	Captain
Major	Major	Major
Oberstleutnant	Lieutenant-Colonel	Lieutenant-Colonel
Oberst	Colonel	Colonel
Generalmajor	Brigadier*	Brigadier-General
Generalleutnant	Major-General	Major-General
General der...**	Lieutenant-General	Lieutenant-General
Generaloberst	General	General
Generalfeldmarschall	Field Marshal	General of the Army

Notes:
* equivalent to *Generalmajor* and brigadier-general, but not a general rank
**rank completed with the arm of service or speciality of the owner
(e.g. Rommel was a *General der Panzertruppen*)
In German, cardinal numbers are shown by a dot after the number,
thus 7. Panzer-Division stands for 7th Panzer Division.

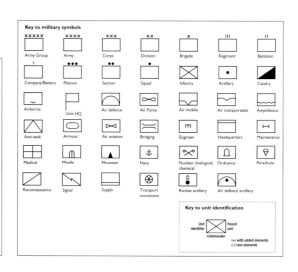

Panzer divisions that fought, and won, the campaign in the West in spring 1940. It was a unique opportunity that enabled Rommel to distinguish himself and paved the way for his appointment as commander of the German Afrikakorps, the assignment that made his name famous all over the world.

There have been many volumes written on the war in the desert and surely more to come. What is clear is that Rommel defined the Axis presence in the theatre – both in the minds of his adversaries and to writers ever since. This has ensured his elevation into that small clique of commanders whose fame is not measured by their battlefield successes or failures. And there were failures. His career in North Africa ended in defeat and he could well have spent the remainder of the war employed in a high-level staff role or in some strategic sideshow. However, his appointment to oversee the defence of Western Europe against the Allied invasion ensured his continuing fame, though only serious injury spared him from defeat in Normandy. However, it did not spare him his eventual fate. Whether he was involved in the plot to assassinate Hitler or not, his decision to commit suicide to avoid trial and repercussions against his family would be the final step in the process of turning the man into a myth. Like Patton, Rommel did not survive the war but has endured in popular imagination as one of the defining commanders of the period. This post-war myth has survived for many years, perpetuated by a mixture of facts and propaganda.

THE EARLY YEARS

Erwin Johannes Eugen Rommel was born at Heidenheim, near Ulm (in the duchy of Swabia, part of the kingdom of Württemberg in south-west Germany), on 15 November 1891, the second of four children – three sons and one daughter. His father, Erwin Rommel, was a teacher of mathematics at a secondary school at Heidenheim (later a headmaster at Aalen) and his mother, Helene von Luz, was the daughter of a local government official. The young Rommel displayed a greater aptitude for outdoor activities than academic studies, though he did show some ability at mathematics. By the time Erwin started his three-year course at Realgymnasium at the age of 16, his fate had already been decided; he would join the army. This was only possible for those who, like Rommel, had an upper-middle-class background, and even then it was not easy.

German officers were recruited at a local level by regiments and, following their training, they were commissioned by the commanding officer following a vote by the other officers. This system ensured that the officer ranks were filled with those of the required social background. The most prestigious units – cavalry or guards regiments – were essentially reserved for members of the nobility or those families with a long tradition of military service. Even Rommel's first choices, the artillery and engineers, were beyond his grasp, and

A German *Stosstrupp* (assault detachment) training on the Isonzo front, October 1917. Their armament includes two British Lewis machine guns. (Private collection)

on 19 July 1910 the young Erwin Rommel became a *Fahnenjunker* (officer candidate) in Infanterie-Regiment König Wilhelm I (6. Württembergisches) Nr. 124 in Weingarten. After eight months of training he was sent to the Kriegsschule in Danzig in March 1911; this was the equivalent of a military academy and gave a standardized course of training to all the officers of the German Army. (There were ten of them across the country, established in 1810.) Rommel graduated on 15 November 1911, having met his future wife, the 17-year-old Lucia Maria Mollin, whom he called Lucie. Back with his regiment, Rommel was commissioned *Leutnant* (second lieutenant) on 27 January 1912 and began training recruits himself.

The concluding remarks of the Danzig Kriegsschule are worth noting; Rommel was average in all areas apart from leadership, in which he was classified 'good'. Rommel's service with IR 124 lasted until 1 March 1914, when he was attached to Feld-Artillerie-Regiment Nr. 49 at Ulm; here he served in the 4. Batterie until 31 July. He was back with IR 124 on 1 August 1914, the day World War I started, and two days later he and his unit left for the Western Front as part of 5. Armee. From 21 August Rommel was in action in the Meuse Valley on the Verdun front, first as a platoon commander then as regimental aide. On 24 September he was wounded in the thigh, hospitalized and on the 30th awarded the Iron Cross second class. He was back with his regiment in January 1915, now commanding its 9. Kompanie, in time to be part of another attack against Verdun. On 29 January he led his company in attack, only to be soon surrounded by the French; through inspired leadership he managed to clear the enemy positions and get back to the German lines. That earned him the Iron Cross first class on 22 March, the first lieutenant of his regiment to receive this award. In June Rommel, now a platoon commander owing to the arrival of a new intake of officers, took part in an offensive in the Argonne; in July he was slightly wounded in the leg, which earned him a spell of leave back home and then, in September, he was promoted to *Oberleutnant* (first lieutenant). In October Rommel was transferred to the newly formed Württembergisches Gebirgs-Bataillon (WGB), a mountain infantry battalion, as a company commander.

Between December 1915 and October 1916 the WGB was based on the Western Front in the Vosges area, then it was transferred to the Romanian front, where Rommel was introduced to a form of warfare he had not encountered before, a war of movement. Shortly after this he took advantage of a short leave to marry Lucie on 27 November. Both the organization of the battalion and the new type of warfare suited Rommel well. With several strong rifle and machine-gun companies, the WGB could be broken up into ad hoc combat groups according to the need of the moment, which led to Rommel often commanding more than a single company. Flexibility, speed and ingenuity all were key elements of the new type of warfare the Germans were testing in the field. Between January and July 1917 the WGB was back on the Western Front, going again to Romania in August where it fought the battle for Mount Cosna. Here, on 9 August, Rommel led an audacious attack with practically the entire battalion. Though he was wounded in the arm in the process, Rommel managed to seize the height and defend it from the counterattack that followed. At the end of August the WGB was pulled out of the line and, after some rest (which Rommel spent with Lucie on the Baltic), sent to Italy in September. Here Rommel's career would have its real beginning.

THE MILITARY LIFE

By late 1917 the German Army had nearly completed a major tactical reorganization. The new *Stosstrupp* tactics were based on deep infiltration of enemy lines, which required inspired, skilled and resolute commanders to enable the breakthrough of enemy positions. With Russia on the verge of collapse a new front was sought where these tactics could be tested, and Italy seemed the perfect choice. If the Germans managed to break through the Italian lines on the Isonzo River and reach Venice, they could then threaten the Po Valley and the heartland of Italy. This might knock her out of the war, and then their forces could shift to the Western Front. An Alpenkorps (mountain corps) was formed, and the WGB, along with the Königlich Bayerische Infanterie-Leib-Regiment, was to storm a key position on the Italian line: the Kolovrat Ridge with its dominating height of Mount Matajur. After breaking through the Italian forward positions on 24 October 1917, on the 25th Rommel led his own detachment up Mount Matajur sweeping aside enemy positions, capturing hundreds of prisoners and getting close to the summit, which was too well defended to capture. Rommel changed the plans for the operation; while elements of

After his promotion to *Generalmajor* on 1 August 1939, Rommel took command of Hitler's HQ during the Polish campaign. Note the 'Führerhauptquartier' cuffband on the left sleeve of Rommel's uniform. (NARA)

Rommel (at left, with the camera hanging from his shoulder) had only three months to acquaint himself with his new command, 7. Panzer Division, before the German attack in the West started. (HITM)

the Königlich Bayerische Infanterie-Leib-Regiment dealt with Mount Kuk, he led four of his own companies down a trail to a valley behind Mount Matajur. Here he took even more prisoners (some 2,000) and rejoined the rest of the WGB, which had seized Mount Kuk and broken through the Italian lines. On the 26th Rommel stormed the nearby mounts Cragonza and Mrzli until the WGB's commander, Major Sproesser, believing the whole area was in German hands, ordered him to withdraw. Knowing his commander was wrong, Rommel disobeyed his order, and, taking some 100 men with him, he attacked the summit of Mount Matajur and seized it, taking hundreds more prisoners. At 11.40am flares were sent up to signal the position had been taken and the enemy defences ruptured decisively.

These events started the battle of Caporetto – a debacle for the Italian Army and a partial success for the German Army, which failed in its major goal of breaking through into the heartland of Italy. However, in the early days of November 1917 that goal seemed to be within their grasp.

On 7 November, having crossed the Tagliamento River, Rommel was ordered to attack an Italian position covering a pass. This attack failed because, as Rommel himself pointed out, while he was busy organizing covering fire from machine guns, the infantry companies delayed their attack. This was not a mistake he would make again. Three days later Rommel's detachment crossed the Piave River and seized the town of Longarone, taking hundreds of prisoners again adding up to a total of over 10,000 since the beginning

River crossing played an essential role during the opening stage of the German attack across Belgium, which started on 10 May 1940, and Rommel was ruthless in using any available pontoon bridges. (HITM)

of the offensive. The Piave marked the limit of German advance. The offensive slowed and eventually came to a halt in November, with the WGB being transferred to the Grappa Massif where it found more determined enemies and was unable break through. In late November the WGB was pulled out of the line, returning on 17 December, and Rommel was granted leave back home. He would not return either to the WGB or to the front as on 11 January 1918 he was given a staff position at the HQ of LXIV Armeekorps.

Rommel was appointed commander-in-chief of the Afrikakorps on 3 February 1941, and on the 12th he arrived at Tripoli. Note how he and the other officers are still wearing European-style uniforms, which were soon replaced by tropical ones. (HITM)

The events of October–November 1917 would affect Rommel deeply, especially the matter concerning the award of Germany's most important decoration: the Pour le Mérite, also known as the 'Blue Max' after one of its earliest recipients in World War I, the air ace Max Immelmann. Rommel discovered accidentally that two other officers had been awarded the 'Blue Max' for the battles on the Kolovrat Ridge: Oberleutnant Ferdinand Schörner of the Königlich Bayerische Infanterie-Leib-Regiment, who seized Mount Kuk, and Oberleutnant Walther Schnieber of Infanterie-Regiment 'von Winterfeldt' (2. Oberschlesisches) Nr. 23. Apparently Schnieber took Mount Colonna (behind Mount Matajur) and reported this to his HQ; however, his message was altered, transforming him into the one who had seized Mount Matajur. The fact that both Schörner and Schnieber, unlike Rommel, belonged to the army's establishment probably had something to do with it. Deeply shaken, both Rommel and Sproesser protested vehemently up to the level of the Kaiser's cabinet. Eventually both were granted the award on 18 December 1918.

On 18 October 1918, shortly before the armistice of 11 November, Rommel was promoted to *Hauptmann* (captain). He was back with IR 124 on 21 December 1918 but, after it was disbanded, left in March 1919 to join Sicherheitskompanie 32 at Friedrichshafen to fight against a local uprising, which he did again in the areas of Müsterland and Westfalen in the spring of 1920. On 18 October he swore allegiance to the Weimar Republic and, on 21 December 1921, joined the new Reichswehr and became commander of 4. Kompanie of IR 13 in Stuttgart.

His achievements and decorations were a key factor in assuring him a position with the new army, along with the fact that its rigid social structure had been definitively broken. The new Reichswehr was 100,000 strong and allowed only 4,000 officers; in 1914 the Reichsheer (Imperial German Army) possessed some 46,000 regular officers. Although some 11,500 of them were killed during the war, getting a job in the new army was extremely difficult, and once in the pace of promotion was extremely slow. The new chief of staff,

A column of PzKpfw IV tanks lined up in the streets of Tripoli, part of 5. leichte-Division's Panzer-Regiment 5. (Carlo Pecchi)

Hans von Seeckt, was looking for officers with a general staff background who were capable of commanding above their actual rank. These abilities would ensure that the Reichswehr would be able to expand quickly once the limitations of the Treaty of Versailles were overcome. The Reichswehr therefore consisted of a strong core of experienced officers supported by a large intake of new officers, who would serve for only a limited period of time. Although the Kriegsakademie, the German Army's staff college, was closed down, the system remained in operation at local level. The fact that Germany no longer had a strong army but retained strong enemies, meant that it was vital that her limited army was a hotbed of innovation and intellectual development. These developments did not suit Rommel and his career stalled.

Like all other officers with 10 years of service, Rommel underwent an examination to test his professional ability. This lasted several days and included writing three different papers on tactics, several others on engineering, map reading and weapons and equipment, as well as answering questions on several subjects including military history, economics, geography, mathematics, physics and chemistry. Failure would result in the officer retaking the exam the following year; a second failure could lead to the officer losing his commission. The top 10–15 per cent were considered for general staff training, with only one in three actually making it through. Rommel was not amongst them, which is hardly surprising given both the selection rate and Rommel's academic aptitude.

The only major event in Rommel's life during these years was the birth of

Rommel, wearing an Italian 'Sahariana' uniform, with General der Flieger Stefan Fröhlich, the 'Fliegerführer Afrika' (Luftwaffe commander in North Africa). (HITM)

A Fieseler Fi 156 Storch, an aircraft Rommel used extensively during the first offensive in Cyrenaica in spring 1941. (HITM)

his son Manfred on 24 December 1918. Finally, on 1 October 1929 Rommel became a teacher at the Infanterieschule at Dresden, a position which enabled him to take full advantage of his experience and knowledge even though, as a colleague of his later recalled, he was not a great thinker. Promoted *Major* on 1 April 1932, on 1 October 1933 he had his first spell of command with III Battaillon of IR 17 at Goslar (the 'Goslarer Jäger'). Here he met Adolf Hitler for the first time on 30 September 1934. On 1 March 1935 Rommel was promoted *Oberstleutnant* (lieutenant-colonel), and a few days later Hitler reintroduced conscription in Germany, which was the beginning of a new army. This brought no immediate change to Rommel's career and on 15 October he became an instructor at the Infanterieschule at Potsdam, which saw him attached to Hitler's military escort during the Nazi party's rally in the summer of 1936. From 7 January 1937 Rommel was without a position until on 25 February he was attached as the War Ministry's liaison officer to Baldur von Schirach, the leader of the Hitlerjugend (Hitler's youth organization),

A typical view from the Storch in April 1941: columns of German vehicles advancing at full speed along a desert track. (HITM)

with whom Rommel had a difficult relationship. That same year Rommel also published his renowned book *Infanterie Greift an* (*Infantry Attacks*) which, other than being a personal recollection, was intended for use at war colleges and academies as a textbook. By 1945 it had sold some 400,000 copies. Promoted *Oberst* (colonel) on 1 October 1937, Rommel met Hitler again between 1 and 9 October 1938, during the German seizure of the Sudetenland, when he commanded the Führerhauptquartier (Hitler's HQ) and escorted him personally. It was probably no coincidence that on 10 November,

Rommel became commander of the Kriegsschule at Wiener Neustadt, a position he temporarily relinquished between 15 and 23 March 1939 to command the Führerhauptquartier once more. Promoted *Generalmajor* (brigadier) on 1 August 1939, on the 23rd (at mobilization) Rommel was again commander of the Führerhauptquartier during the campaign against Poland. Early in 1940 Hitler asked him what command he would like to have, and Rommel replied without hesitation: a Panzer division.

On 12 February 1940 Rommel took over command of the 7. Panzer-Division, which had been formed on 18 October 1939 from the 2. leichte-Division (a mixture of cavalry and armour) commanded by Generalleutnant Georg Stumme, who in September–October 1942 briefly replaced Rommel as commander of Panzerarmee Afrika. Of the ten commanders of Panzer divisions at the time, Rommel was the only one to have commanded neither a brigade nor a division, and also the only one not to see service during the Polish campaign.

Rommel's 7. Panzer-Division attacked across Belgium towards the Meuse on 10 May 1940, crossing in the area of Dinant. They advanced along with the 5. Panzer-Division, as both were part of Hermann Hoth's XV Armeekorps. By 12 May a bridgehead was established across the river, and, on the 15th, Rommel attacked westwards breaking through the French positions and smashing the bulk of French 1ère Division blindée in the process. In the early hours of 17 May the 7. Panzer-Division was across the Sambre River, like Guderian's Panzer divisions farther south. He then drove towards Cambrai (18 May) reaching Arras on the 20th; here on 21 May Rommel's 7. Panzer-Division faced the only major counterattack launched by the Allies after the German breakthrough. Led by British Matilda tanks it spread havoc amongst the Germans, though the situation was eventually restored and the counterattack repulsed with the loss of 36 Matildas.

On 23 May the division was at the Aa Canal, on the southern portion of the Dunkirk Pocket. Because of Hitler's 'halt order' the attack was not launched until the 26th and, the following day, the division was across the canal attacking towards Lille. At the end of May, before the surrender of the remnants of the Allied forces in the pocket, the 7. Panzer-Division was pulled out of the line and Rommel counted his booty: 6,849 prisoners, 48 tanks captured and another 313 destroyed.

The second part of the campaign in the West started on 5 June, with Rommel's 7. Panzer-Division attacking across the Somme between Amiens and Abbeville. After fierce fighting to break through the French defences, by 10 June the division had reached the sea at the port of St Valéry, between Dieppe and Le Havre, where elements of an entire French corps and the 51st British Division surrendered on the 12th, with 12,727 prisoners being taken by the 7. Panzer-Division, a dozen generals included. On the 17th the division set out towards Cherbourg, which was reached on the 18th after an advance of some 240km (150 miles) in a single day. Fortress Cherbourg surrendered on 20 June, the following day the French signed an armistice with the Germans. Rommel's 7. Panzer-Division had captured 97,648 men, 277 field guns, 64 anti-tank guns, 458 tanks and armoured cars and more than 4,000 lorries since 10 May. Its losses were higher than any other Panzer division: 682 killed, 1,646 wounded and 296 missing, plus 42 tanks permanently destroyed. On 17 and 21 May Rommel was awarded the 1939 clasps to his first- and second-class Iron Crosses, followed by the Knight's Cross on 27 May.

Rommel's career might have taken quite a different path had it not been for chance. Following Operation *Compass* in North Africa, which led to the British seizure of Cyrenaica and the destruction of an Italian army, Hitler decided to send a 'blocking formation' to prevent from British advancing to Tripoli. On 3 February 1941 Hitler replaced Hans von Funck with Rommel as the commander of the German force destined for Africa, which was at the same time increased to an entire corps, becoming the Deutsches Afrikakorps on 19 February. On 7 February Rommel was promoted *Generalleutnant* (major-general), and on the 12th he set foot on Africa's soil for the first time. He would spend two years here waging a see-saw campaign that would earn him fame and the nickname of the 'Desert Fox,' not to mention both promotions and decorations. Once Cyrenaica was reconquered, Rommel was

The central part of Rommel's defence plan against the threatened Allied invasion was the deployment of all the available Panzer divisions close to the threatened coast. (HITM)

awarded the oak leaves to his Knight's Cross on 20 March and on 1 July he was promoted *General der Panzertruppen* (lieutenant-general); on 15 July Panzergruppe Afrika was formed with him in command. After the Axis forces were driven from Cyrenaica in December 1941, Rommel attacked again in January 1942 stopping only when he reached the defences of Tobruk. This second drive earned him the crossed swords to the Knight's Cross on 20 January and, on 30 January, promotion to *Generaloberst* (general), which coincided with the renaming of Panzergruppe Afrika as Panzerarmee Afrika. In May 1942 Rommel attacked the British Gazala Line in a battle that ended with the fall of Tobruk – which earned him promotion to *Generalfeldmarschall* (field marshal) on 22 June 1942 – and the drive to El Alamein, where the Axis forces would be beaten in November. After the retreat to Tunisia, on 23 February Rommel was given command of the newly formed Heeresgruppe Afrika, which he held until 9 March when left for Europe. On 11 March he was awarded the diamonds to his Knight's Cross.

On 15 July 1943 Rommel was given another command, that of Heeresgruppe B in northern Italy shortly before Mussolini's downfall and Italy's exit from the war. The idea was for him to take command in this new theatre, but eventually Hitler choose Kesselring instead and on 5 November Rommel was sent to northern France, first as inspector of the coastal defences and then, from 1 January 1944, as commander of Heeresgruppe B in north-west Europe. This put him once more on the front line when, on 6 June, the Allies landed in Normandy. On 17 July Rommel was wounded in an air attack on his car and was evacuated to Germany. Here he committed suicide on 14 October following his involvement in the plot to assassinate Hitler.

THE HOUR OF DESTINY

The professional soldier

'No plan survives contact with the enemy's main body;' General Helmuth von Moltke's (chief of the Prussian Großer Generalstab, 1857–88) most famous quote embodies the root concepts of the modern German way of war. As the situation on the battlefield changes often and swiftly, detailed and meticulous planning is likely to be close to useless as it will not react to developments in a timely way. Not that Moltke dropped planning completely, rather he emphasized the initial deployment of forces and approach to the battlefield (*Aufmarsch*). However, he knew well that flexibility, based upon individual initiative, was the only way to deal with the changing situation on the battlefield. That led to the concept of *Auftragstaktik* – mission tactic – which is not so much a tactical system as a method of command. Once a goal or a mission had been set out, the commander explains it to his subordinates while leaving them the choice of how to attain it using their own methods and means, and taking into account the forces available. Commanders were thus required to appreciate the situation quickly and correctly, making their own decisions and implementing them with appropriate orders to their own subordinates.

Early in the 20th century, long-established tactical systems imposed a level of restraint on this command system. When Rommel was a cadet German infantry was still trained according to the 1906 manual, which did not differ much from the 1888 version. While support weapons like machine guns and artillery were taken into account, infantry was still the 'queen' of the battlefield. An assault required strong lines of riflemen in close order (up to battalion level) gainimg 'fire superiority' over the enemy in order to shock him into submission, following which infantry occupied the ground.

By the end of 1914 it became clear these concepts were largely outdated. In order to regain freedom of movement on the battlefields of the Western Front, a new tactical system was devised from 1915 onwards based on the *Stosstrupp*, or assault troops. This system was based on small combat groups (*Kampfgruppen*) operating with a variety of weapons and equipment, as well as close artillery support. These groups would act independently, searching for holes in the enemy's defensive lines, getting though them and then storming the enemy positions either from the flanks or the rear, or even bypassing them and attacking the supply and communication lines in rear areas. Regular units would then attack and break through the front, creating the premises for a major breakthough. These tactics were first tested on the Eastern Front and then at Caporetto before being used on a large scale on the Western Front in spring 1918. They brought back to the battlefield the concepts of manoeuvre, speed, movement and flexibility so dear to Moltke. However, this would not have been possible without the concept of *Auftragstaktik* spreading down the ranks to junior officer level. This way officers like Rommel found themselves spearheading major offensives and proving their worth on the battlefield despite their lowly social status. This was the beginning of the end for the Prussian Army, and the birth of the German one.

Post-war German Army doctrine, heavily influenced by General Hans von Seeckt, would be spread by the manual *Führung und Gefecht der verbundenen Waffen* (*Combined Arms Command and Battle*, 1921), later revised in 1936 as the well-known *Truppenführung* (*Command of Troops*). Commanders, at every level, were now the key element of battle in the *Auftragstaktik* system; orders were still orders in the German Army, yet as Seeckt put it in 1921 'If the mission no longer suffices as a basis for action, or has been superseded by events, then the decision [of the commander] must take account of these conditions.' This is what Rommel had done as a young *Leutnant* as early as 1914–15. The *Truppenführung* of 1936 states:

> The situations arising out of war are infinitely varied. They change often and unexpectedly and can rarely be foreseen in advance,... The emptiness of the battlefield demands independently thinking and acting fighters who exploit each situation in a considered, determined, and bold way.... Habituation

to physical effort, hardness against oneself, willpower, self-confidence, and courage enable a man to master the most difficult situations. The quality of commander and men determines the fighting power of a unit which must be properly backed up by high quality supply and maintenance. High fighting power can cancel out numerical inferiority. The higher this quality, the stronger and more mobile the conduct of war.

A comparison between the German doctrine and Rommel's writings and actions will reveal how close the two were; according to the *Truppenführung*, *Auftragstaktik* was a command system based on mission and situation, with the former consisting of the objective to be attained and the latter being any hurdle likely to arise while accomplishing it: 'Confusion concerning the situation is the normal state of affairs. Only rarely will exact details about the enemy be known. While the attempt to find out about him is a matter of course, waiting for news in a difficult situation is a bad error.' Commanders, at every level, had to take into account the crucial factors of modern warfare: decisiveness, speed and flexibility, and so '... favourable situations [can be] quickly recognized and exploited with determination.' Taking into account that 'Surprise is a crucially important means to bring about success'. For that reason the German command system was quite straightforward; orders had to be simple, short and fast, often issued only verbally, and they had to be carried out taking into account that every commander was working '... within the framework of the whole'. Which meant that commanders were to take into account the situation on the battlefield and, if the situation changed or proved different from expectations, alter their mission and report about it to their superiors, taking responsibility for the consequences. Since the best way to appreciate the situation on the battlefield is to observe it first hand, German commanders stressed the concept of 'leading from the front', getting as close as possible to the front line to assess the situation. This was a concept particularly dear to Rommel, who wrote 'In my view the duties of a commander are not limited to his work with his staff. He must also concern himself with details of command and should pay frequent visits to the fighting line...' (*The Rommel Papers*, p. 226).

But leading from the front was not the sole criterion for success from Rommel's point of view. Once again concepts like speed and decisiveness would emerge in the thinking of a German general:

> One of the first lessons I had drawn from my experience of motorised warfare was that speed of manoeuvre in operations and quick reactions in command are decisive. Troops must be able to carry out operations at top speed and in complete co-ordination. To be satisfied with norms is fatal. One must constantly demand and strive for maximum performance, for the side which makes the greater effort is the faster – and the faster wins the battle. Officers and NCOs must continually train their troops along these lines.
>
> *The Rommel Papers*, p. 225

Speed was certainly the principal component of Rommel's approach to warfare. Writing about the 1940 campaign, he commented: 'The sole criterion for a commander in carrying out a given operation must be the time he is allowed for it, and he must use all his powers of execution to fulfil the task within that time' (p. 119). And again: 'The officers of a Panzer Division must learn to think and act independently within the framework of a general plan and not wait until they receive orders' (p. 17). Such a way of thinking created quite a few a problems with his subordinate commanders who, from his point of view, were not capable of that 'habituation to physical effort, hardness against oneself, willpower, self-confidence, and courage' that enabled 'a man to master the most difficult situations' stressed in the *Truppenführung*. Rommel was, and he required the same levels of ability from his subordinates. This is clearly evident in the notes Rommel made about modern military leadership while recovering from the injuries suffered on 17 July 1944:

> The tactical leader of the future, who will decide the battle – for the main emphasis of future battles will be on the tactical destruction of the enemy's fighting power – will need not only mental gifts of a high order, but also great strength of character if he is to be a match for his task. Because of the great variety of tactical possibilities which motorisation offers it will in the future be impossible to make more than a rough forecast of the course of a battle. This being so, the issue will be decided by flexibility of mind, eager acceptance of responsibility, a fitting mixture of caution and audacity, and the greater control over the fighting troops.
> *The Rommel Papers*, p. 517

The field commander

Without any doubt Rommel had a talent for appreciating the situation quickly and reacting accordingly. The way he dealt with the situation he and his company, 9./IR 124, had to face on 29 January 1915 clearly shows how the young Rommel did not differ greatly from the older, experienced one. At first the attack seemed simple; the company, moving to the left of the neighbouring III Bataillon, quickly seized three series of French defensive lines without problems, largely because the French were withdrawing. After advancing for 1.5km (1 mile), Rommel and his men found another French fortified position, heavily protected by wire entanglements. This time, seeing his men reluctant to follow him, Rommel was forced into desperate measures. He got hold of his leading platoon commander and simply told him 'obey my orders instantly or I'll shoot you'. This worked and the company was soon inside four French blockhouses, with the wire to their backs. At this point, the French started to fire at them from the flanks while a large force started to attack 9. Kompanie's positions; Rommel requested for support, but this was not forthcoming and the company was surrounded and forced to withdraw. As Rommel recorded, he faced three options: fight to the last round and then surrender, try and make his way back through the wire,

Leading from the front was a key part of Rommel's concept of command throughout his entire career. Here he is checking maps with officers from 7. Panzer-Division during the early stages of the German attack in the West in May 1940. (NARA)

which almost certainly meant heavy losses, or attack. And attack he did, spreading confusion and disorder among the French who, once their lines had been ruptured, proved unable to keep up with the fast pace of Rommel's company. Eventually, they managed to get through the French defensive lines, cut a passage through the barbed wire and rejoin the rest of II Bataillon for the cost of five wounded. Rommel's comment was that it was unfortunate that no one had been able to exploit his company's success.

Although Rommel may appear to have taken a gamble, he would not have seen it that way. German officers were trained to evaluate the situation and react swiftly taking the enemy by surprise, not to gamble. Years later, writing about the war in North Africa, Rommel pointed out the difference:

> It is my experience that bold decisions give the best promise of success. But one must differentiate between strategical and tactical boldness and a military gamble. A bold operation is one in which success is not a certainty but which in case of failure leaves one with sufficient forces in hand to cope with whatever situation may arise. A gamble, on the other hand, is an operation which can lead either to victory or to the complete destruction of one's force. Situations can arise where even a gamble may be justified – as, for instance, when in the normal course of events defeat is merely a matter of time, when the gaining of time is therefore pointless and the only chance lies in an operation of great risk.
> *The Rommel Papers*, p. 201

Rommel was a bold commander, not a gambler. The battle for the Kolovrat Ridge and the advance that followed are perfect examples of Rommel's application of his battlefield talents, and it must rank as one of his finest achievements as a field commander. Again, Rommel appreciated the situation at first hand, driving himself and his men over difficult terrain in the face of the enemy, making bold decisions and overcoming all obstacles.

A few days after the Kolovrat Ridge, Rommel experienced the changing nature of warfare in an episode that was to shape his future career. On 7 November, he led his men forwards to attack an Italian position on a mountain pass from which they were firing against the advancing German columns. He took three rifle and one machine-gun companies up the mountain by a circuitous route. The rifle companies were supposed to launch the attack while the machine guns provided covering fire. However, Rommel spent too long with the machine-gun company setting up their fields of fire and was late in joining his rifle companies. Although the machine guns were providing covering fire, the attacking force waited for Rommel to join them and, by the time the attack was launched, the covering fire had died away. Rommel's subordinates had failed to live up to the high standards that he set both for himself and for them. This led him to a simple conclusion: if he wanted to be sure of success he needed to keep everything under his personal control.

Owing in part to this, Rommel's relationships with his subordinates could often be difficult. From the moment he joined the 7. Panzer-Division in February 1940, he complained about his officers who preferred an 'easy life,' describing some of them as 'floppy'. Less than two weeks after his arrival, Rommel had a clash with a battalion commander who was forced to leave the very same day to set an example for the others. Things were also not easy in North Africa, and it was only 'Later in the campaign, when I had had a chance to establish closer relations with the troops', that he discovered how 'they were capable at all times of achieving what I demanded of them' (*The Rommel Papers*, p. 119). As was Rommel's custom, he was often in the front lines, something he deemed necessary because:

> Accurate execution of the plans of the commander and of his staff is of the highest importance. It is a mistake to assume that every unit officer will make all that there is to be made out of his situation; most of them soon succumb to a certain inertia. Then it is simply reported that for some reason or another this or that cannot be done – reasons are always easy enough to think up. People of this kind must be made to feel the authority of the commander and be shaken out of their apathy. The commander must be the prime mover of the battle and the troops must always have to reckon with his appearance in personal control.
> *The Rommel Papers*, p. 226

This is some way beyond 'leading from the front'. Rommel, while being very keen on applying the *Auftragstaktik* concept to orders from above and 'independently thinking and acting' as stressed in the *Truppenführung*, also exercised such tight control over his subordinate commanders and units that he practically wiped out any independent thought or deed. From his own experience, Rommel was clearly convinced that such a method of command was vital at a battalion level, and he applied the same principles to divisional command.

When he took command of 7. Panzer-Division in February 1940 Rommel had only limited experience as a field commander. He had commanded

The Meuse at Dinant was the first obstacle in the advance of 7. Panzer-Division. Before a pontoon bridge was built, Rommel used ferries to get his Panzers across the river, which proved to be a decisive step. (HITM)

only infantry battalions or battalion-sized units previously, and had gained no experience during the 1939 campaign against Poland. In particular, he had never had any experience at all with either motorized or mechanized units. Many other commanders would have considered all these factors as a major hurdle and relied on their staff and subordinate commanders to a great extent. Rommel did not, and, despite the risks involved in this approach, it all worked out well for him. When the German offensive on the Western Front opened on 10 May 1940, Rommel had been in his new command for less than three months, yet within a few weeks his remarkable achievements and the speed with which the division kept moving during its advances would earn it the nickname 'la division fantôme' (the ghost division). As a German historian has recently noted, he led his Panzers like an infantry storm troop of World War I – using the same infiltration tactics he had employed as an infantry *Leutnant*. He had problems from the very beginning with the neighbouring 5. Panzer-Division, whose bulk lagged behind Rommel's division – apart from an advanced armoured detachment that was put under Rommel's command. It was this unit, only temporarily part of 7. Panzer-Division, which established a bridgehead across the Meuse a few kilometres north of Dinant late on 12 May. Rommel eventually split his division into two for the crossing, with one motorized infantry regiment to the north, along with the 5. Panzer-Division, and another motorized infantry regiment with the Panzer regiment to the south, at Dinant. The latter's attempt to get across the river on 13 May saw Rommel performing the role of field commander to perfection; always at the front, he sent Panzer units forwards, coordinated fire support and even arranged for new assault rafts. However, without heavy fire support the attempt failed – once again, according to Rommel, because of the actions of his subordinate officers, who were appalled by the heavy losses and unwilling to press forwards. The following morning, with the divisional artillery now in range, Rommel made another attempt, this time taking personal command of the assault battalion and crossing the Meuse with one of the first assault rafts. Once a bridgehead had been established, Rommel had the divisional engineers building a ferry and then a pontoon bridge, which enabled the first Panzer to get across the river by morning of the 14th.

Blitzkrieg in the West, May 1940

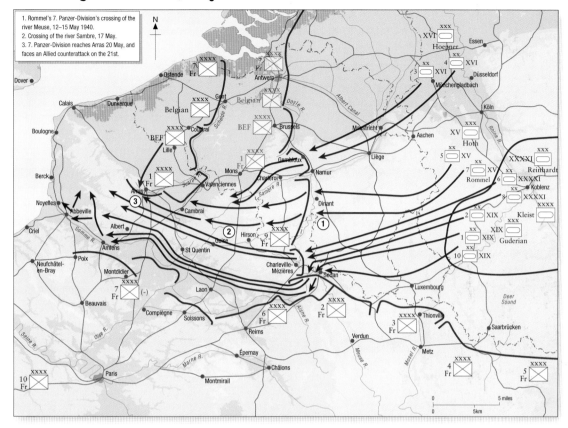

1. Rommel's 7. Panzer-Division's crossing of the river Meuse, 12–15 May 1940.
2. Crossing of the river Sambre, 17 May.
3. 7. Panzer-Division reaches Arras 20 May, and faces an Allied counterattack on the 21st.

Once across the Meuse, Oberst von Bismarck, commander of Schützen-Regiment 7, put himself at the lead of the advanced elements of his unit and probed towards the town of Onhaye, some 5km (3 miles) from the southern bridgehead. At 8.00am a message was received from his unit before communications broke down: Bismarck was surrounded at Onhaye. Without hesitation Rommel took all the available Panzers and advanced towards Onhaye with the aim of placing '… the Panzer Regiment itself in a wood 1,000 yards north of Onhaye and then to bring all other units up to that point, from where they could be employed to the north, north-west or west, according to how the situation developed' (*The Rommel Papers*, p. 12).

Approaching the southern edge of Onhaye, Rommel came under enemy fire with his tank being hit twice; a strike on the periscope wounded Rommel in the right cheek, nothing serious but it bled a great deal. 'The driver promptly opened the throttle wide and drove straight into the nearest bushes. He had gone only a few yards, however, when the tank slid down a steep slope on the western edge of the wood and finally stopped, canted over on its side, in such a position that the enemy, whose guns were in position about 500 yards away on the edge of the next wood, could not fail to see' (*The Rommel Papers,* p. 12). Apart from the tank, there was not much change from his experiences on Mount Cosna or the Kolovrat Ridge. Once again Rommel survived his clash with the enemy and, after fierce fighting, his units seized Onhaye to discover that Bismarck's message had been misunderstood and his unit had not been surrounded (*eingeschlossen*), but had simply reached (*eingetroffen*) Onhaye. By late evening, 7. Panzer-Division's spearheads had broken through the French second line of defence, driving a 12km-deep (7-mile) wedge into it, while a second bridge on the Meuse was completed. Rommel had broken through the enemy front in a similar manner to the way he had in 1917. There was, however, an important difference: even Rommel realized he could not be everywhere and thus had to rely on modern communications. These would play a key role in his new position as a divisional field commander and, again, were used in a decisive, speedy and flexible way. To avoid time-consuming coding and decoding, Rommel used the simple and ingenious system based on the *Stosslinie* (thrust line) – a line drawn on the map to which all units referred using a simple code. That made communications in the clear possible, all kept short and simple in the true spirit of *Auftragstaktik*. An example would be Rommel's request for a situation report sent at 5.50am on 13 May, a simple 'Wie Lage?' (how's the situation?), which was answered with: '0600 S[chützen] R[egiment] 7 Fluss Maas überschritten' (river crossed at 6.00am). On 14 May Rommel's order to advance was again a simple 'Rommel 1930 Verfolgung mit allem Waffen', 'Rommel at 7.30pm: pursuit with all weapons'. Rommel himself stressed the role played by radio communications in ensuring tight control of his division, while all the time he led from the front.

> A tight control west of the Meuse, and flexibility to meet the changing situation, were only made possible by the fact that the divisional commander with his signal troop kept on the move and was able to give his orders direct to the regiment commanders in the forward line. Wireless alone – due to the necessity for encoding – would have taken far too long, first to get the situation reports back to Division and then for Division to issue its orders. Continuous wireless contact was maintained with the division's operation staff, which remained in the rear, and a detailed exchange of views took place early each morning and each afternoon between the divisional commander and his Ia [staff officer, operations]. This method of command proved extremely effective.
> *The Rommel Papers*, p. 13

This was in fact the method used throughout the German Army, and especially by the Panzer divisions. Rommel was a more ardent exponent than most, mainly owing to his pronounced desire to lead from the front. In fact, his command skills during the campaign in the West, especially for an inexperienced infantry commander, compare very well with the more renowned and esteemed 'Panzer General' Guderian, who delayed his crossing of the Meuse at Sedan by waiting until a pontoon bridge was built before moving his tanks across the river, while Rommel moved his tanks across by ferry until his pontoon bridge became available, which enabled him to break through the French defences. Rommel's first test as a divisional commander, and a Panzer commander, was passed with flying colours.

However, he also showed his lack of interest in cooperating with other commanders, and thinking and acting 'within the framework of a general plan'. During the crucial hours of the Meuse crossing, there was equipment available for only one heavy pontoon bridge. Rommel asked and eventually obtained from the corps commander, General Hoth, that it was put at his disposal, much to the displeasure of General von Hartlieb of 5. Panzer-Division. To add insult to injury, 5. Panzer-Division's heavy tanks crossed the river by use of Rommel's bridge, and he took the chance to put them under his command without asking permission. It was at this stage that Rommel and the commander of 5. Panzer-Division's Panzer-Regiment 15, Oberst Johannes Streich had a major argument that led to mutual antipathy.

Rommel was awarded the Knight's Cross on 27 May 1940, and on 5 June his 7. Panzer-Division started its drive across France as part of the German offensive that ended with the French surrender. In the background is a PzKpfw II light tank from regimental HQ. (HITM)

Although it is true that the neighbouring 5. Panzer-Division was slower than Rommel's own 7. Panzer-Division, and Hartlieb was relieved of command on 21 May and given an administrative role, Hartlieb was also correct in his complaints to Hoth that 7. Panzer-Division could not always fight alone, and should operate more as part of the corps. Hoth may not have been particularly happy with Rommel's methods of command but, realizing that he did not have enough tanks available to support two breakthroughs, was left with no other choice but to support him.

One other point about this campaign that is worth mentioning is the feeble nature of the opposition. The French were unable to organize a timely counterattack, and therefore Rommel's 7. Panzer-Division was able to regroup on the morning of 15 May and set out from its forward positions, now some 10km (6 Miles) west of Onhaye. To the north the French 1ère Division blindée was regrouping and preparing a counterattack following a long march. Had this unit launched its attack the previous evening it would have stormed the positions of the unprepared leading elements of 7. Panzer-Division. However, the heavy French tanks were not designed for travelling long distances and they were compelled to wait for the arrival of tank transporters. On the morning of 15 May they had started the long and complicated process of refuelling when Rommel's 7. Panzer-Division attacked them.

Rommel's advance cut the French supply route and the division itself was actually destroyed by the neighbouring 5. Panzer-Division. At times, this is what makes the difference between a bold action and a gamble: a feeble enemy. This is precisely what Rommel faced again on 21 May at Arras, when his division alone faced the British and French counterattack; the neighbouring 5. Panzer-Division was delayed, and his own 7. Panzer-Division was dispersed over some 25km (16 miles) with the armour leading and the infantry following up behind. When the British Matilda tanks, invulnerable to any German anti-tank weapon, advanced upon the German infantry they came close to collapse and disaster was avoided only by the faulty British command system, which meant there was no senior commander at the front, combined with Rommel's presence in the front lines. His presence stiffened the resolve of his troops and they were able to hold the line. The German defences were broken through twice, but there was no panic. Rommel was able to set up a new forward defence line with light anti-tank and anti-aircraft guns. Although these were unable to harm the Matildas, they halted the accompanying light tanks. At the same time, a main defence line was arranged with artillery and heavy anti-aircraft guns, the famous 88mm, which destroyed some 20 tanks in a few minutes. The intervention of the Luftwaffe and the recall of 7. Panzer-Divisions' Panzer regiment put a definitive end to the counterattack. The field commander had won the battle.

Desert warfare

In 1940–41 no one fighting in the North African desert had any experience of mechanized warfare in the theatre. The Italian commander in Libya, Maresciallo Graziani, took inspiration for his advance into Egypt from Kitchener's campaign in the Sudan, while the British general O'Connor started his own offensive, which led to the destruction of Graziani's army and the conquest of the whole of Cyrenaica, as a limited counterattack intended to relieve the Italian pressure against Egypt. In early January 1941 Hitler, facing the threat of an Italian collapse in the region, decided to send a German blocking formation to help them, and this Germans force was the least experienced of any of the combatants. Their knowledge of the desert was limited to an inspection tour of a few days by the inspector of armoured troops, General von Thoma, in October 1940 and to the knowledge of General Kirchheim, who served in the German central Africa colonies during World War I. Rommel, who was eventually chosen by Hitler to lead the Afrikakorps, possessed few of the qualifications required for the job. Though successful, his term of command in charge of a Panzer division had been short, while he had fought the Italians during World War I.[1] He had also not done much to win sympathy among the German officer community. Instead his methods of command had come in

Rommel checking a map with Tripoli Harbour in the background. Given the size of the map, it would appear he was already thinking of an advance towards Egypt! (HITM)

---

[1] It is worth noting that many of the traditions of the Afrikakorps were derived from the German Alpenkorps of World War I. Rommel did not inform the Italians of this.

The campaign in Cyrenaica, 1941

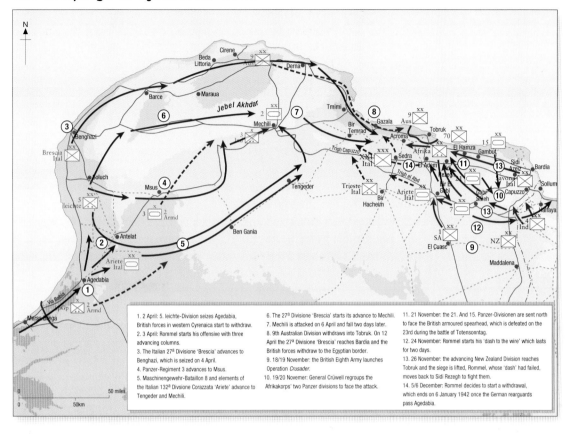

1. 2 April: 5. leichte-Division seizes Agedabia, British forces in western Cyrenaica start to withdraw.
2. 3 April: Rommel starts his offensive with three advancing columns.
3. The Italian 27ª Divisione 'Brescia' advances to Benghazi, which is seized on 4 April.
4. Panzer-Regiment 3 advances to Msus.
5. Maschinengewehr-Bataillon 8 and elements of the Italian 132ª Divisione Corazzata 'Ariete' advance to Tengeder and Mechili.

6. The 27ª Divisione 'Brescia' starts its advance to Mechili.
7. Mechili is attacked on 6 April and fall two days later.
8. 9th Australian Division withdraws into Tobruk. On 12 April the 27ª Divisione 'Brescia' reaches Bardia and the British forces withdraw to the Egyptian border.
9. 18/19 November: the British Eighth Army launches Operation *Crusader*.
10. 19/20 November: General Crüwell regroups the Afrikakorps' two Panzer divisions to face the attack.

11. 21 November: the 21. And 15. Panzer-Divisionen are sent north to face the British armoured spearhead, which is defeated on the 23rd during the battle of Totensonntag.
12. 24 November: Rommel starts his 'dash to the wire' which lasts for two days.
13. 26 November: the advancing New Zealand Division reaches Tobruk and the siege is lifted, Rommel, whose 'dash' had failed, moves back to Sidi Rezegh to fight them.
14. 5/6 December: Rommel decides to start a withdrawal, which ends on 6 January 1942 once the German rearguards pass Agedabia.

for much criticism, as had his sending of a nicely bound copy of a narrative of his division's achievements during the campaign in the West to Hitler.

The complexities of the new theatre of war were apparently clear to Hitler and the army staff. There would be no strengthening of the German forces in North Africa until the end of the war against the Soviet Union, thought to be in the winter of 1941–42, and then an offensive towards Egypt could be undertaken. Rommel was authorized to move the Axis defence lines forwards, which meant attacking towards Agedabia by mid-May (after the arrival of the Afrikakorps' second division, the 15. Panzer-Division) and to prepare for an attack against Tobruk for the following autumn, but only once a favourable ratio of forces had been built up.

Prior to this German troops had to get to know their new theatre of war and train accordingly. Forces had to be concentrated in order to achieve maximum force at the *Schwerpunkt*, the point of main effort that could bring about the destruction of the enemy forces in the field, which was the basic requirement for an advance against Egypt to be successful. Supplies were a problem too; everything had to be carried by sea across the Mediterranean and, once unloaded at the port of Tripoli, moved forwards using lorries. An evenly paced advance to a suitable jump-off point would have enabled the creation of a network of supply dumps that would have

greatly shortened the logistic chain's distance from the forward units. However, Rommel had other ideas.

Two days after Rommel's arrival in Libya, on 14 February 1941 the first German units arrived at Tripoli. Rommel wasted no time and sent them forwards, and by the end of the month an advanced defence line had been established at some 25km (16 miles) from El Agheila. Rommel's plan was to attack towards Tobruk early in May, a plan that neither Hitler nor the army staff agreed to. Returning to Libya on 24 March from a series of meetings in Germany and Italy, Rommel discovered that Generalmajor Streich, commander of 5. leichte-Division, had captured El Agheila and undertaken an armed reconnaissance towards Mersa el Brega, which was the easternmost limit of Rommel's area of operations, and a suitable base for future offensives.

On 31 March Streich attacked and seized Mersa el Brega after a fierce battle, the following day a reconnaissance towards Agedabia was planned but, rather than sending just a detachment, Streich put the entire division on march. Agedabia was seized on 2 April, but this victory proved unpopular with the high command. The Italian commander to whom Rommel was formally subordinated, warned against moving the front too far forwards, and the German high command clearly stated that any further advance could be undertaken only if the enemy was evacuating Cyrenaica on its own. Facing only a weak defence on the British side, Rommel took the decision to undertake a 'bold operation'. Taking 5. leichte-Division and two Italian divisions under command (the armoured 'Ariete' and the partly motorized 'Brescia'), he launched an offensive on 3 April using his familiar *Stosstrupp* tactics and aiming for the fortress port of Tobruk.

The advance was organized in three columns: the German Auflärungs-Abteilung 3 and the 'Brescia' division advanced towards Benghazi; Panzer-Regiment 5 moved towards Msus; the third one, consisting of Maschinengewehr-

Bataillon 8 and elements of the 'Ariete' division, advanced towards Tengeder and El Mechili deep in the desert. The British forces simply collapsed, with the 2nd Armoured Division practically melting away, and the pace of the Axis advance soon became exhilarating. Benghazi fell on the 4th, Derna was seized on the 6th and El Mechili was taken two days later. The road to Tobruk was open, and now Rommel began to tell his soldiers that the final objective of the operation was the Suez Canal. On 12 April Aufklärungs-Abteilung 3 reached Bardia, while the British mobile forces withdrew to the Egyptian border and the 9th Australian Division withdrew to Tobruk and fortified the perimeter.

In retrospect Rommel's first African victory was flawed; he overestimated the capabilities of his own forces and underestimated his enemy's abilities, being fooled into thinking the British were disintegrating as opposed to giving up space for time. Despite his unceasing efforts and his driving forwards from the front, his troops were lacking both the experience and the training for desert warfare, becoming disorientated during the advance across featureless terrain, getting stuck and running out of fuel. Tobruk became a thorn in the side of the German position. Garrisoned by 30,000 determined Australians, the fortress was not something Rommel could overcome with his own inexperienced and understrength forces. The first two attempts, made on 11 and 12 April, were unsuccessful while the first major attack on the 13–14th was repulsed once the defensive perimeter had been broken through. All following attempts to storm Tobruk were unsuccessful as well, including one led personally by Rommel on 18 April and a major attack

The Royal Navy made the task of bringing supplies and reinforcements across the Mediterranean extremely difficult. The situation was a great concern for Rommel who, throughout the campaign, demanded increased efforts and often complained about the inadequacy of the logistical support for his Panzerarmee Afrika. (HITM)

As suggested by the Luftwaffe eagle sported on the t-shirt of the soldier on the right, this was not an army HQ. However, it is a typical installation common throughout North Africa, and is a good illustration of the conditions in which staff had to work: exposed to heat, protected only by canvas. (HITM)

The crew of a PzKpfw III tank checking the sky for Luftwaffe aerial support. As Rommel would experience first hand, air supremacy over the battlefield was an essential prerequisite for success, and when the Royal Air Force won it in Egypt during the summer and autumn of 1942 the Axis forces lost a good deal of their capability to manoeuvre. (Carlo Pecchi)

on 30 April–1 May at Ras el Mdauuar (carried out using elements of the fresh 15. Panzer-Division). Losses increased, supplies became scarce and morale collapsed. However it rose again owing to a combination of British counterattacks and German intelligence. The counterattacks against the Sollum position on 15–16 May (Operation *Brevity*) and 15–17 June (Operation *Battleaxe*) were easily repulsed by the Germans, taking advantage of their superiority in mobile, mechanized warfare, not to mention the fact that the Afrikakorps' intelligence service had provided advance notice of both. However, the time was ripe for a major reorganization of Axis forces in North Africa and Rommel's own command.

On 15 July Panzergruppe Afrika was formed under Rommel's command, with the Afrikakorps and two Italian army corps at its disposal. A third, motorized German infantry division ('Afrika', later 90. leichte Division) began to arrive and, while Rommel planned a new assault on Tobruk, the German army staff started planning for an offensive towards Egypt. However, with German forces now fighting against the Soviet Union no reinforcements were available, and the African offensive had to be a long-term plan; the attack on Tobruk was scheduled for September, that towards Egypt for March 1942. The attack against Tobruk was delayed and the British offensive came first, on 19 November. The battle that followed the launch of the British Operation

The battle of Totensonntag

On the afternoon of 23 November 1941, the German Totensonntag or 'Sunday of the dead,' armoured and mechanized elements of the 15. and 21. Panzer-Divisionen stormed the positions held by the 5th SA Brigade from the south. The Germans attacked with all their tanks and vehicles firing on the move (a common German tactic), taking the enemy by surprise and annihilating the 5th SA Brigade while inflicting serious losses on the British 22nd Armoured Brigade when it counterattacked. Rommel took this as a decisive victory and decided to start his 'dash to the wire.' A PzKpfw III (left) and a PzKpfw II (right) of 15. Panzer-Division's Panzer-Regiment 8 move past a destroyed lorry while advancing north to Sidi Rezegh.

Rommel checking a map with a group of officers during the battle of Gazala, May–June 1942. This was one occasion where his command and leadership would make the difference and lead to an Axis victory. (HITM)

Rommel aboard his SdKfz 250/3 command vehicle 'Greif' watching the battlefield through binoculars. To his right is Oberst Fritz Bayerlein who was chief of staff of the Afrikakorps from October 1941 to November 1942. (HITM)

Crusader (known to the Germans as the 'Winterschlacht') was a confused affair, with many mistakes on both sides. Rommel was caught off guard, partly because of an intelligence failure that gave no warning of the attack, and his reactions were slow and uncertain. For two days he thought that the enemy attack was not a major offensive, and appeared on the battlefield only on the 21st at Belhamed to fight the enemy armoured drive. The burden of the battle fell on the shoulders of the commander of the Afrikakorps, Generalmajor Ludwig Crüwell, who for four days had no contact with Rommel. However, he successfully regrouped the two Panzer divisions, swung them to the south and then sent them in a drive north against the enemy spearheads at Sidi Rezegh. On the 22nd Rommel sent his orders to Crüwell, which the latter dismissed because he found them 'excessively detailed', then he put himself at the head of the Panzer divisions and on the 23rd these forces succeeded in inflicting serious losses to the enemy forces south of Sidi Rezegh, in what became known as the battle of Totensonntag (the Sunday of the dead). This caused a crisis on the British side and the Eighth Army commander, Cunningham, wondered whether to continue with *Crusader* or not. Rommel had no doubts – the enemy had suffered decisive losses and he now wanted to complete its destruction with a drive to the Egyptian border to destroy the Eighth Army supply lines and cut off its retreat. Early on the 24th Rommel explained his plan to Crüwell, who suggested a more conservative solution: chase the enemy forces and clear the area east of the frontier. Rommel disagreed, and told Generalmajor Johann von Ravenstein (who had replaced Streich in command of the 5. leichte, now 21. Panzer-Division), 'You have the chance to bring this campaign to an end this night'. In the words of the German official history, what followed bore little resemblance to a solid general staff military operation.

As 15. Panzer-Division was delayed and did not show up in time at the starting position, Rommel launched his 'dash to the wire' with

21. Panzer-Division alone. It was soon caught up in a series of running battles with British forces and by the evening its forces were spread over 70km (44 miles). However, its spearheads had reached the border at 4.00pm, and by the evening 15. Panzer-Division was only some 35km (22 miles) from the border. Rommel, the chief of staff of Panzergruppe Afrika, Generalmajor Alfred Gause, and Crüwell spent the night beyond the border, in Egypt. For the following two days the 'dash to the wire' turned into a series of uncoordinated actions without any specific aim and with orders

Generalleutnant Walther Kurt Nehring, commander of the Afrikakorps from 9 March to 31 August 1942, relaxing with a group of officers. Wounded on 31 August, Nehring would return to Africa in November as commander of Stab Nehring in Tunisia. (HITM)

coming from three different sources: some actions were simply led by Rommel who gave his orders on the spot. Communications with the HQ of Panzergruppe Afrika were hampered by the fact that Rommel's messages referred to a *Stosslinie* unknown to his HQ, and were therefore incomprehensible. There was panic among the British forces, but Rommel managed to miss Eighth Army's HQ as well as its advanced supply bases, the British advanced airfields also remained intact. On the 26th the British forces in Tobruk and the advancing New Zealand forces linked up at Ed Duda; the encirclement was broken and Rommel ordered the two Panzer divisions to withdraw the following day. The 'dash to the wire' achieved nothing beyond adding further strain and losses to the German forces. Between 30 November and 2 December the Afrikakorps counterattacked in the breakthrough area, but was unable to surround Tobruk again. The turning point of the battle came when, between 5 and 6 December, Rommel

A PzKpfw III tank moving past a burning British lorry. During the early years of the campaign in North Africa German tanks were badly armed and armoured in comparison with some of their British counterparts, this Ausf. G shown here has a 50mm short-barrelled L/42 gun and 30mm thick frontal armour. (Carlo Pecchi)

was informed that supplies would be minimal until January and that only scant reinforcements were available for him in Germany. At this point Rommel decided to withdraw west of Tobruk, to the Gazala Line, and asked for permission to withdraw the Axis forces from Sollum. This was denied and they eventually surrendered in January 1942. On 15 December the British forces attacked the Gazala Line, and Rommel decided to withdraw further west abandoning all of Cyrenaica. An organized retreat, logistical troubles on the

Hauptmann Wilhelm 'Papa' Bach, a Lutheran pastor who took command of I Battalion, Schützen-Regiment 104 in April 1941 and which distinguished itself at the Halfaya Pass. Bach was awarded the Knight's Cross on 9 July 1941. Left behind following Rommel's retreat in December 1941, he and his men surrendered on 17 January 1942; Bach died in captivity on 22 December 1942. (HITM)

side and the arrival of 45 tanks, which enabled Crüwell to counterattack the British armoured spearheads on 28 and 30 December inflicting the loss of 60 tanks at the cost of 14 of his own, prevented a disaster like the one the Italians had faced one year before.

On 6 January 1942 the last German rearguards left Agedabia, and on the 22nd Rommel was on the move again; his second drive into Cyrenaica had started. Once more the British forces were caught off balance, but in the early stages they succeeded in escaping the trap and on the 25th the German forces were at Msus. Mussolini asked Rommel not to advance any further, but again Rommel ignored orders from above. Taking advantage of the uncertain situation, the Afrikakorps attacked towards Benghazi on the 29th while a feint was aimed at Mechili. The capture of Benghazi and the destruction of an Indian brigade opened up the road to Tobruk once more. Immediately after his promotion to *Generaloberst* on the 30th, Rommel attacked along the coastal road while the British forces withdrew. On 6 February the advancing German forces halted right before the British defence line at Gazala. This time Rommel stopped and the offensive was over.

Rommel made several mistakes in the first part of his campaign in North Africa, and learned many lessons from it: 'The experience which I had gained during this advance through Cyrenaica formed the main foundation for my later operations. I had made heavy demands throughout the action, far more than precedent permitted, and had thus created my own standards' (*The Rommel Papers*, p. 120).

He had made heavy demands indeed. The decision to strike early to take advantage of enemy weaknesses could well have been the right one, but only if it led directly to the decisive victory that military planners in Germany had been seeking. What Rommel achieved was a half-baked victory that then developed into a stalemate, leading eventually to the successful British counteroffensive. The first, and largest, mistake was a simple one: Rommel did not take into account the condition of his own troops. They lacked adequate training, and had not acclimatized and become accustomed to the desert. Therefore they still were not effective enough and failed both to move fast enough to prevent the Australians from withdrawing into Tobruk and to storm it effectively thereafter. Also, with the bulk of the Afrikakorps still in the process of being transported to North Africa, the Axis forces lacked strength and were unable to seize the fortress which, come winter, would be

For most part of the North African campaign, Rommel was to rely on improvisation and captured equipment. Here a column is led by an Opel Blitz lorry with a four-barrelled 20mm anti-aircraft gun, a Flakvierling 38, mounted on its chassis. It is followed by a captured British Ford truck. (Carlo Pecchi)

the ultimate cause of their defeat. Rommel would blame his subordinate commanders for the training deficiencies of his troops, which he considered the reason behind the failed attack at Ras el Mdauuar ('The high casualties suffered by my assault forces were primarily caused by their lack of training.' *The Rommel Papers*, p. 133), but he carefully overlooked the fact that this was a consequence of his premature decision to attack, first into Cyrenaica and then against Tobruk, before reinforcements had arrived and could accustom themselves to an unfamiliar environment. Because of his 'heavy demands' his over-stretched forces were unable to train, because they were too busy with front-line duties.

Supplies were a constant issue, a recurring factor during the North African campaign. First of all there was the problem of bringing them across the Mediterranean and unloading them in Tripoli, a remote and unsuitable port. Then they had to be brought forwards to the battlefield, generally through the use of motor transport. Rommel is often criticized for being unconcerned about the logistical situation, but this is not strictly accurate.

Rommel made extensive use of command and staff cars. Worth noting in this photo is Rommel's leather overcoat, which he wore with a civilian scarf given to him by his sister, and a bullet hole barely visible on the back of this Mercedes Benz Kfz 15, suggesting it got too close to the enemy. (HITM)

Rommel was greatly concerned about his logistical situation, at least for the overseas transportation, as demonstrated by the records and by his own writings. However, in much the same was as many other German generals, he could not allow logistics to hamper field operations, and it was someone else's concern to deal with them Rommel would thus demand and expect the impossible, but he would not allow logistics to put a curb on his plans.

The same Kfz 15 staff car, showing the table fitted inside to check maps. The officer seated to Rommel's right is Oberstleutnant Eduard Crasemann, an artillery officer who became commander of 15. Panzer-Division in 1942, 26. Panzer-Division in Italy in 1943–45 and XII SS-Korps just before Germany's surrender in 1945. Awarded the Knight's Cross on 10 January 1942 and the oak leaves on 18 December 1944, after the war he was sentenced to ten years' imprisonment for the alleged execution of Italian partisans and died in prison in 1950. (HITM)

Rommel awarding Afrikakorps' soldiers with the Iron Cross second class. His energy and willpower would soon win him the sympathies of his men. (HITM)

The field marshal

In winter and spring 1942 the German forces in North Africa completed the process of reorganization started the previous summer. New units were set up, troops were trained and supply dumps completed. This was possible thanks to the creation of the staff of Panzergruppe Afrika (Panzerarmee Afrika from 30 January 1942). Command and staff issues had bedevilled the German forces during the first year of the campaign, with the small Afrikakorps staff proving inadequate for its needs. From this point onwards, command was one of the trump cards of the German forces in North Africa. In contrast to the position on the British side, the Germans benefited from a great deal of continuity at the highest levels of command, with Rommel nearly always in charge (he was replaced by General Ludwig Crüwell for ten days in March 1942 and by generals Georg Stumme and Wilhelm von Thoma between late September and late October), and with some of the finest general staff officers around him. These included the chief of staff of Panzergruppe/Panzerarmee Afrika, Generalmajor Alfred Gause (temporarily replaced by Afrikakorps' chief of staff, Oberst Fritz Bayerlein, in summer 1942) and Oberstleutnant Siegfried Westphal, who was Rommel's operations officer (Ia) until October 1942, though he was temporarily replaced during the summer by the intelligence officer (Ic) of the Panzerarmee, Major Friedrich W. von Mellenthin. The Afrikakorps enjoyed a similar continuity; Crüwell, who took over from Rommel on 15 August 1941, was in charge until early March 1942 and then replaced by one of Germany's most renowned Panzer commanders: Generalleutnant Walther K. Nehring. Another famous Panzer commander, General der

Panzertruppen Wilhelm von Thoma, took command on 17 September. (Bayerlein took over again in November after he was captured.) Divisional commands saw many more changes, principally because of losses.

In May 1942 the Axis forces in North Africa were at their highest point. A strategic plan for the Mediterranean had been devised – Rommel was to strike first in North Africa and seize Tobruk, immediately after this the planned air–sea assault against Malta would take place to ensure the security of naval supply routes in the Mediterranean. The plan of attack against the Gazala Line bore the hallmark of classical German military doctrine with the mobile forces concentrated in a sweeping movement south of the enemy defence line, then moving behind it on the open ground. Again, as typical with German planning, there were no specific goals. The plan consisted of detailed routes of march and target areas, leaving the commander on the ground the task of evaluating the situation at first hand and reacting accordingly. However, Rommel also gave his own personal twist to the plan. According to his own 'rules of desert warfare' non-motorized infantry only had value against motorized and armoured enemy forces when it occupied prepared positions, however, since from his perspective the British forces were fully mobile, their annihilation by encirclement was not possible. They could, on the other hand, be forced to evacuate their areas and fight in the

Battle of Gazala, May–June 1942

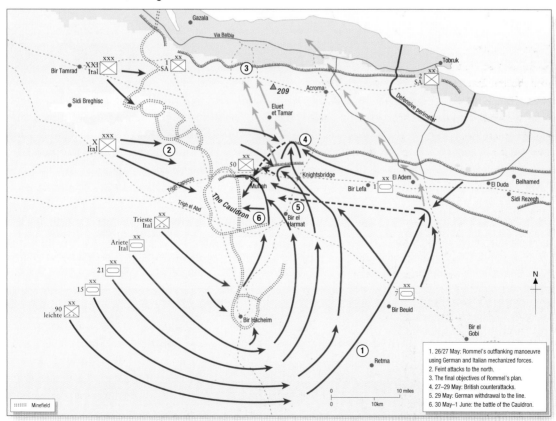

1. 26/27 May: Rommel's outflanking manoeuvre using German and Italian mechanized forces.
2. Feint attacks to the north.
3. The final objectives of Rommel's plan.
4. 27–29 May: British counterattacks.
5. 29 May: German withdrawal to the line.
6. 30 May–1 June: the battle of the Cauldron.

Checking the battlefield from the only feature available in the desert: a tank turret. Rommel's style of command combined with the environmental conditions took a heavy toll on the men of the Afrikakorps. Casualties were high, particularly amongst officers, as were sickness rates. By the summer of 1942 Rommel reckoned he still had with him only half of those who arrived in 1941. (Carlo Pecchi)

open, which is where Rommel wanted them to be. In an opposite scenario to that taking place on European battlefields, Rommel believed that encirclement could only lead to the destruction of the enemy forces when their lack of supplies had made them immobile or because of inadequate command or heavy losses. Since sealed pockets were hard to achieve in the desert, the first was an unlikely occurrence, 'The encirclement of the enemy and its subsequent destruction in the pocket can seldom be the direct aim of an operation; more often it is only indirect, for any fully motorized force whose organisational structure remains intact will normally and in suitable country be able to break out at will through an improvised defensive ring' (*The Rommel Papers*, p. 199).

Annihilation was to be achieved rather by 'battles of attrition, battles in the open aimed at destroying the fighting power of the enemy by wearing down their *matériel* and breaking their cohesion'. These battles, fought 'with the highest possible degree of mobility' (*The Rommel Papers*, p. 199), required concentration of forces in order to isolate portions of the enemy's force and defeat them in detail. Essential requirements included the preservation of one's own supply lines, the use of armour as main spearhead, effective field reconnaissance, concealment of one's own intentions and 'Speed of movement and the organisational cohesion of one's own forces' (*The Rommel Papers*, p. 200).

Rommel would call his plan Operation *Theseus*, and he launched it on the night of 26 May against the Gazala Line. This was a bold decision and possibly the closest thing to a gamble he ever tried. Thanks to their training the German divisions marched at night to the south of the line, outflanked it and the morning after appeared between El Adem and Acroma. For a while it looked like German forces had marched into a trap and at this point Rommel took over, and the German method of command proved its superiority over the British one. Having appreciated the situation at first hand, Rommel decided to alter his plan completely and try another approach. After three days of battle he ordered mobile forces to withdraw westwards to secure his supply routes and establish a defensive line against British mobile forces. The 'battle of the cauldron' saw Rommel opening a supply route to the west and repulsing British counteroffensives, each committed piecemeal and ending with severe losses. By 11 June the second major stronghold on the line, Bir Hacheim, was in Axis hands and finally, on 12–13 June, Rommel fought the decisive battle in the open that opened the way to Tobruk. Between 17 and 19 June Tobruk was encircled again, this time

Rommel's car, an Italian Alfa Romeo 2500 coloniale, is a clear example of recycling: first in use with the Italian army, as denoted by the license plate reading Regio Esercito, it entered Afrikakorps service, was given the typical palm and swastika symbol and, as denoted by the tactical insignia on the right mudguard, was used by the staff of Panzergruppe Afrika. (HITM)

with no chance of holding out, and stormed on the 20th with the garrison surrendering the following day, a huge source of booty for the Axis forces and Rommel's greatest victory. With the enemy forces apparently annihilated and their remnants withdrawing eastwards, Rommel saw again the same opportunity that flashed through his mind while advancing into Cyrenaica during the previous spring: the Suez Canal and a decisive victory in North Africa. The day before his promotion to *Generalfeldmarschall*, and even before Hitler gave him a green light on the 24th Rommel set the Afrikakorps en route to the Egyptian border, while at the same time abandoning the planned assault on Malta. By 26 June the Axis forces were at Mersa Matruh, where Rommel won another victory and resumed his advance to the canal on the 28th. Two days later the British forces withdrew to the El Alamein Line, which was attacked on 1 July following the same pattern as the attack at Gazala: a breakthrough of the enemy defence line with the aim of bringing its forces to battle in the open where they would be destroyed piecemeal. The first attempt to break through the Alamein Line failed, and the Australian counterattack on 10–11 July brought the first serious setback of the campaign, with the Italians collapsing in the north. From this point onwards Rommel was to face failure.

Rommel with Generalmajor Bernhard Hermann Ramcke, commander of the Luftwaffe's Ramcke Brigade, intended for use on Malta and then deployed at El Alamein. (HITM)

The battle of Alam Halfa (for the Germans Second Alamein) of 30 August–6 September 1942 was a pale attempt at executing another breakthrough battle in the manner of Gazala. With the Panzerarmee now exhausted and lacking supplies, Rommel had no chance of winning. Once more his 'tremendous' (as he

The *Generalfeldmarschall* inside a staff car, talking with his commanders. Rommel's face clearly shows signs of strain and physical exhaustion. (HITM)

called them) demands had been well beyond the capabilities and the conditions of his own troops, he had also underestimated the capabilities of the enemy forces, the harshness of the terrain and climate in the Egyptian desert and his overstretched supply lines, which added further strain to an already troublesome logistical situation. Reading Rommel's own account, the problems of inadequate supplies and of the physical endurance of his men are clearly evident, as are the reasons behind the failure at Alam Halfa: lack of supplies and enemy air superiority. In September 1942 Rommel, according to his papers, realized the campaign could not be won at El Alamein unless adequate supplies and reinforcements were provided; they were not. The overly optimistic mood he displayed while in Germany, where he went on 23 September to recover from illness caused by his prolonged stay in Africa, was just circumstance and an attempt to 'bring some postponement to the British offensive' (*The Rommel Papers*, p. 295).

Fatal hours: meeting in the desert

Rommel, wearing a leather overcoat with a civilian scarf given to him by his sister, meets his commanders in the field just before the decisive armour battle of 12–13 June 1942 at the Knightsbridge defensive box. The group in the foreground includes generals Walther Nehring (**1**) and Georg von Bismarck (**2**); Oberst Fritz Bayerlein is attending (**3**). Nehring, seen wearing the tropical version of a motorcyclist's overcoat, was commander-in-chief of the Afrikakorps between 9 March and 31 August 1942, when he was badly wounded during an air attack and sent back to Germany. Bismarck was killed in the same ill-fated attack against the Alam Halfa ridge when his command tank exploded. Bismarck, an outstanding tactical leader and probably the best divisional commander in North Africa at the time, had been a motorized infantry regiment commander with Rommel's 7. Panzer-Division in France in 1940 and, after having served on the Eastern Front in 1941, was sent to North Africa at Rommel's request and took over command of the 21. Panzer-Division on 11 February 1942. Nehring was chief of staff of Guderian's corps in 1939–40 until he became commander of the 18. Panzer-Division and fought on the Eastern Front in 1941, before being transferred to North Africa. Between November and December 1942 he took command of the Tunisian bridgehead, being sent back to the Eastern Front in February 1943. There he eventually became commander-in-chief of 1. Panzerarmee on 19 March 1945, before being placed in the reserve on 3 April. Bayerlein, who like Bismarck is wearing the tropical uniform of the Afrikakorps, was chief of operations in Guderian's corps (later *Panzergruppe*) until late 1941 when he was sent to North Africa where he served mainly as chief of staff of the Afrikakorps. In January 1944 he was given command of the Panzer Lehr Division, a task that overwhelmed him. Behind the group stand Rommel's SdKfz 250/3 (**4**) and Bismarck's SdKfz 251/3 (**5**) command vehicles.

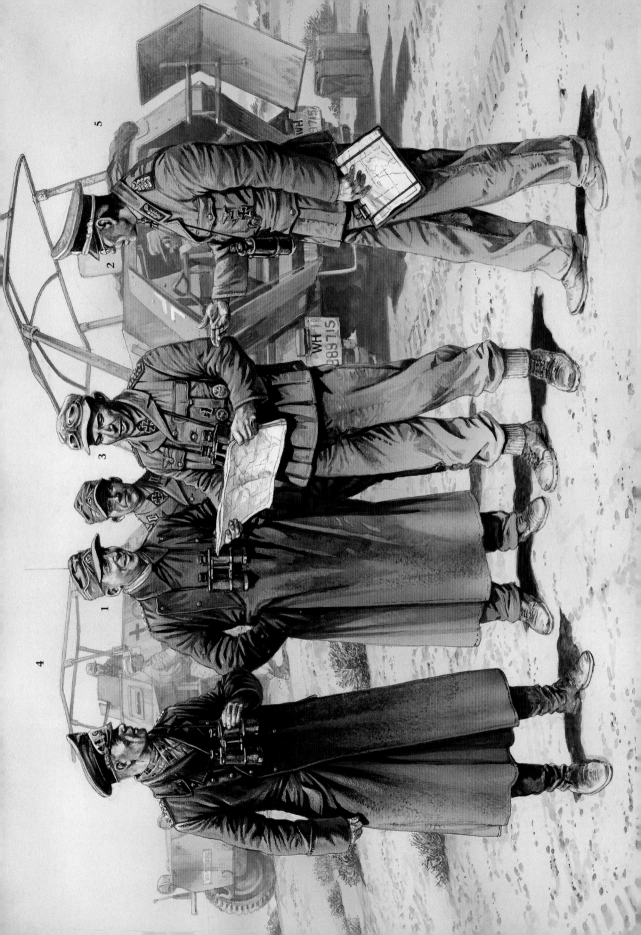

A Panzer column in Tunisia, early 1943, with a heavy Tiger I tank followed by a PzKpfw III. Rommel would spend only one month in this new theatre, leading the unsuccessful attack at the Kasserine Pass. (Carlo Pecchi)

However, Rommel also considered that he might inflict a serious enough defeat on the forthcoming British assault that the whole balance would be shifted. The defences at El Alamein were structured according to the typical German tactical doctrine, a pattern Rommel would also implement some time later in Normandy. It consisted of a rigid defence based on a static line, heavily fortified and mined, manned by the infantry who had the task of standing fast and repulsing the enemy attacks. Whenever a breakthrough occurred, mobile armoured forces would intervene to counterattack and re-establish the situation on the defence line. This was a solid strategy suited to the terrain and, as Rommel pointed out, imposed by the lack of supplies and of mobility of the Axis forces. The decisive attack at Alamein started on 23 October and, on Hitler's order, on the evening of the 24th Rommel returned to the Panzerarmee. The first phase of the British offensive seemed to play into the hands of the Axis forces, but when the second phase was unleashed on 27 October it soon became clear that the enemy superiority in numbers and firepower was going to overwhelm the Axis position.

On the evening of 2 November Rommel realized how desperate the situation was and ordered a staged withdrawal to the Fuka Line, but the following day got a message from Hitler ordering him to stand fast at Alamein, giving no alternative between victory or death. Rommel was deeply shocked by this order and struggled with it for more than a day until, early in the afternoon of 4 November, he ordered the Panzerarmee to withdraw no matter what. That marked the beginning of a retreat, skilfully managed by Rommel, which ended on mid-February 1943 when the Panzerarmee Afrika settled into the defensive positions of the Mareth Line in Tunisia, where the Axis forces established a bridgehead in November following the Allied invasion of the French north-west African colonies on 8 November 1942. It was soon clear that the Axis presence in North Africa was coming to an end, as demonstrated by the short-lived attack at Kasserine Pass on 19–22 February 1943. The following day Rommel was given command of the newly formed Heeresgruppe Afrika, which he held for a fortnight. On 9 March he was back to Germany on account of his health, leaving Africa for ever. His Afrikakorps survived only two more months.

The image of Rommel after the end of the North African campaign is that of a broken man. The capitulation of Axis forces in Tunisia on 13 May sent him spiralling into a state of depression, and only on 23 July was he given command of a *Heeresgruppe* intended to defend Greece from Allied invasion. Mussolini's downfall

two days later brought a change of destination, and by the end of July he was in northern Italy in charge of Heeresgruppe B. Following the Italian surrender on 8 September 1943 his forces seized the whole area, disarming hundreds of thousands of Italians, in about a week. Rommel hoped to have command of the whole of Italy, but his plan of defence disappointed Hitler. Because of the exposed flanks of the Italian Peninsula, Rommel wanted to withdraw to northern Italy where an elastic defence could be conducted. On 19 October Hitler was about to appoint him but changed his mind, and command in Italy went to Generalfeldmarschall Albert Kesselring, whose delaying defence was exactly what Hitler had in mind. Rommel and part of his staff were sent to northern France on 5 November 1943, at first with the task of supervising the construction of fortifications on the Atlantic Wall, then as commander of Heeresgruppe B in north-west France.

A Luftwaffe 20mm Flakvierling 38 on a self-propelled mount in Normandy, 1944. By this stage anti-aircraft artillery was the main tool available to the Germans to counter the ever-increasing threat posed by Allied air superiority. (HITM)

A German armoured column on the move in Normandy, June 1944. Heavy use of foliage to protect against the Allied air attacks was of little use during the day, and often units had to move using the cover of darkness thus delaying their arrival at the front. (HITM)

Rommel's activity as inspector of the fortifications along the Atlantic coast brought him back to where he was of best use – the battlefield. Relentlessly, Rommel travelled all along the 2,600km (1,600 miles) of the Atlantic coast to check, order, suggest and improve an enormous defence line, which to a large extent existed only on paper. He brought many innovations, like the adoption of shore and inland obstacles against sea and air landing, and under his control both the number and quality of fortifications increased at a rapid pace. That was a double-edged sword, however, as Rommel put every available man to work improving the defences, thus sacrificing valuable training time for a force in the West that was already unprepared. The chain of command in the West was also much more complex than Rommel had experienced before, and now he was to deal both with a direct superior – Generalfeldmarschall Karl Gerd von Rundstedt who, as Oberbefehlshaber West (Commander-in-Chief West), was in charge of the whole of France, and the commander of Panzergruppe

Battle of First Alamein, July 1942

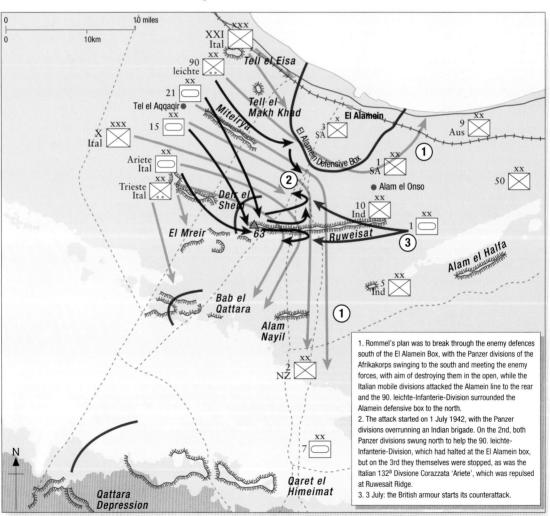

1. Rommel's plan was to break through the enemy defences south of the El Alamein Box, with the Panzer divisions of the Afrikakorps swinging to the south and meeting the enemy forces, with aim of destroying them in the open, while the Italian mobile divisions attacked the Alamein line to the rear and the 90. leichte-Infanterie-Division surrounded the Alamein defensive box to the north.

2. The attack started on 1 July 1942, with the Panzer divisions overrunning an Indian brigade. On the 2nd, both Panzer divisions swung north to help the 90. leichte-Infanterie-Division, which had halted at the El Alamein box, but on the 3rd they themselves were stopped, as was the Italian 132ª Divsione Corazzata 'Ariete', which was repulsed at Ruwesait Ridge.

3. 3 July: the British armour starts its counterattack.

The defence of Normandy, June–July 1944

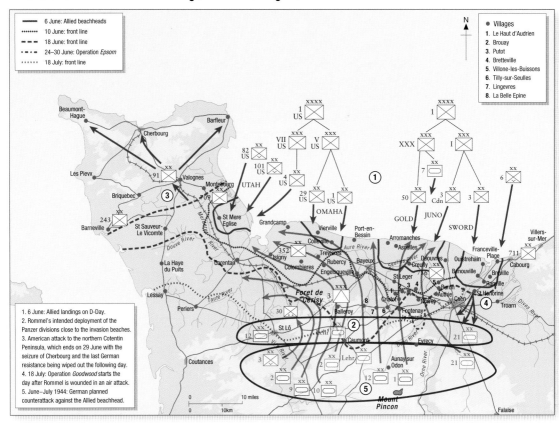

West, General der Panzertruppen Leo Geyr von Schweppenburg.[2] It is hard to think of a worse arrangement for someone who was used to not only dealing directly with Hitler, but who also had nothing in common with two 'old guards', aristocratic officers whose approach was quite different to that of Rommel. Their differences would come to a head with their respective opinions about the deployment of the Panzer divisions.

Following standard German tactical doctrine, both Rundstedt and Schweppenburg wanted to deploy the Panzer divisions inland, with the aim of concentrating them in a massive counterattack against the Allied forces once the 'centre of gravity' of their effort had been identified. This was the classical German flexible defence doctrine that emphasized concentration of forces, movement and manoeuvre over the battle of attrition based around a rigid, static defence line. This was not a view that Rommel agreed with. Based upon his own experiences, and the failure of the German counterattack against the Allied landings at Anzio in Italy, he came to the

---

[2] Geyr von Schweppenburg had been army attaché in London, briefly commanded the 3. Panzer-Division during the Polish campaign and was later a corps commander on the Eastern Front. Hitler considered him a defeatist, and the only positive note for Rommel was the appointment of Alfred Gause as his chief of staff.

As commander of Heeresgruppe B Rommel was responsible for the entire of north-west Europe but, in spite of the large number of units under command, he kept up his habit of frequently inspecting his formations. (HITM)

conclusion that overwhelming Allied air power (as he experienced first hand in North Africa) would deny the Germans those movement and manoeuvre capabilities that were the basic requirements of flexible defence. He proposed a similar defensive pattern to that used at El Alamein: a fixed, prepared defence line strengthened by fortifications and obstacles intended to repulse the enemy assault. Mobile forces were held back to deal promptly with any breakthrough in order to re-establish the defensive line. With the Panzer divisions held close to the landing beaches, swift counterattacks could be launched before the enemy could start its build-up, like at Anzio. Thus, even small-scale operations could prove effective and, by avoiding large-scale movements and concentration of forces, the effects of enemy air superiority could be reduced. Therefore Rommel wanted to deploy the

Panzer divisions close to the most threatened landing beaches, namely those in the Pas de Calais and Normandy, ready to counterattack immediately after the Allied troops started their landings, while their forces were still weak and disorganized and before a build-up race could be started. By counterattacking within the first 24 hours after the invasion, Rommel hoped to prevent the creation of a major Allied beachhead and from

During the battle for Normandy the Germans deployed a large number of armoured and mechanized units, but were never able to concentrate them into a single, decisive counterattack against the Allied bridgehead. Shown here is a self-propelled Sturmgeschütz III, also used as a tank-hunter. (HITM)

here thwart the enemy plans for the invasion. The ultimate solution was an unsatisfactory compromise. Rommel was allowed to deploy three divisions out of ten, which were located between Amiens and Caen (with only one able to counterattack on 6 June, the day of the Allied landings in Normandy); all the others remained as a general reserve at the disposal of Oberbefehlshaber West, though their employment required Hitler's authorization.

Rommel's solution has been often praised as the one that might have helped the Germans to win the battle for Normandy. However, at a closer look it had significant flaws. As the German counterattack at Mortain in August 1944 proves, even in the summer of 1944 the Germans still possessed the capability to concentrate their forces and manoeuvre against the Allies, even though they enjoyed the advantages of full mobility and air superiority over the battlefield. The failed counterattack launched by 21. Panzer-Division against the British beachheads on 6 June 1944 also shows that Rommel's plan for immediate counterattacks against the enemy landings was difficult to put into practice. Given the state of confusion that reigned on the German side in the first hours of the invasion owing to the lack of information, it was hard for the commanders on the ground to assess the situation properly and react

A column of *Panzergrenadiere* from 1. SS-Panzer-Division 'Leibstandarte Adolf Hitler', his personal bodyguard. This division, and many others, would be kept close to the Calais area until late July– August 1944. In the foreground is a SdKfz 250/1 armoured personnel carrier. (HITM)

One of the results of the German doctrine, which favoured manoeuvre over firepower, was the insufficient development of artillery. A solution was found in the innovative use of rocket launchers called *Nebelwerfer* (smoke throwers), which were used to a large extent in Normandy. (HITM)

accordingly. Generalmajor Edgar Feuchtinger, commander of the rebuilt 21. Panzer-Division (the only one close to the coasts of Normandy), launched his attack at first against the British airborne bridgeheads and only turned against the beachheads later on, with the result that the feeble and uncoordinated German attacks achieved nothing. It would have required a Rommel, or indeed more than one, to carry out this plan in a purposeful way. However, by the spring and summer of 1944 the German Army was running short of skilled and experienced field commanders. The real mistake made by the German commanders in Normandy, including Rommel, was to commit their reserves in a piecemeal way. They did this for two reasons; first in an attempt to secure the front line and prevent the Allies from breaking out of the beachheads; second because many, with Rommel amongst them, believed firmly that Normandy was not the 'centre of gravity' of the Allied invasion. This mistake also arose as a consequence of the lack of combat-worthy front-line units, the Panzer divisions being the only ones available, and out of the 'yield not one inch of ground' state of mind that now dominated the German Army. Only after the Allied forces broke through the Normandy beachhead did the Germans attempt to regain the initiative through the use of mobility and manoeuvre. However, by this point it was too late to make

Counterattack on D-Day

Rommel's plan to counteract the Allied landings was to deploy the Panzer divisions close to the invasion beaches, ready to counterattack immediately after the landings. On 6 June 1944 only the 21. Panzer-Division was close to the Allied landing in Normandy, and its counterattacks started only in mid-morning and were uncoordinated. In the afternoon Panzer-Regiment 22 attacked towards the Périers Ridge supported by the infantry of Panzergrenadier-Regiment 192; at Biéville II/Panzer-Regiment 22 lost eight PzKpfw IV tanks to anti-tank guns, while the other battalion had no better luck as it ran into British armour. At dusk the attack was called off, without any breakthrough being achieved.

A Luftwaffe gunner loading an 88mm Flak 36/37, part of III Flak Korps. This gun, like those in North Africa, was employed in Normandy in the dual role of anti-aircraft and anti-tank and soon acquired a sinister reputation amongst Allied tank crews. (HITM)

A German anti-tank rocket launcher, based on the American 'bazooka', called the *Panzerschrek* (tank terror) in Normandy. By late 1943 the widespread introduction of portable anti-tank rocket launchers improved the capability of the German infantry to deal with enemy armour, though it could not close the gap between German tank production and that of the Allies. (HITM)

good their mistakes. The piecemeal commitment of German mechanized reserves in Normandy led to a battle of attrition, different from those fought by Rommel in North Africa, and one that the Germans could not win. The large-scale counterattack against the Normandy beachhead planned in June–July by Panzergruppe West never materialized, simply because all the forces needed were already committed here and there on the battlefront to prevent enemy breakouts.

One can easily imagine how Rommel might have led that counterattack, but the reality was quite different. During the 40-odd days he was active on the Western Front, Rommel visited the front line often to meet unit commanders at every level, giving orders, talking to them and making suggestions. This time there were no offensives or dashes forwards for him to lead, and eventually, as the Allied noticed, it was difficult to make out Rommel's mark on the battle of Normandy. Just as the Normandy of 1944 was something completely different from the North Africa of 1941–42, so the Rommel of 1944 was a different man. The situation had changed, and he was certainly concerned about other matters when, on 17 July 1944, strafing British fighter-bombers hit his staff car in Normandy, putting an end to his military career. The wounded Rommel would not return to the front before his suicide three months later. The military commander was dead, but the myth was about to be created.

A group of *Fallschirmjäger* and a Sturmgeschütz in the Cotentin Peninsula, June 1944. The failure to prevent the seizure of Cherbourg by American forces was the first signal of how desperate the situation in Normandy was. (HITM)

OPPOSING COMMANDERS

'Victory in battle… never comes solely as the result of the victor's planning. It is not only the merits of the victor that decide the issue, but also mistakes on the part of the vanquished. This rule can be applied to the African theatre of war. It was British mistakes, dating back in many cases to before the war, that made our victories possible' (*The Rommel Papers*, pp. 519–20). This is the most acknowledgement that Rommel would give to one of the factors that contributed to some of his most famous successes on the battlefield: his enemy. Things might well have taken quite a different turn if, on 6 April 1941, the advancing German troops had not captured two British generals: the commanders of Cyrenaica Command and the British Forces in Egypt. The latter was General Sir Richard Nugent O'Connor, a career officer commissioned in 1910 who was an instructor at Sandhurst and at Camberley. He had been a divisional commander in the Middle East from 1938, and was familiar with the Mobile Division (later 7th Armoured Division) which had been raised and trained by General Sir Percy Stanley Hobart, one of Britain's first and finest experts in armoured warfare, and would provide the bulk of those forces that defeated the Italians. O'Connor became commander of the Western Desert Force (XIII Corps from 1 January 1941) in June 1940, and led it in the victorious offensive that started at Sidi Barrani in December 1940 and ended two months later at Beda Fomm with the destruction of an entire Italian army. O'Connor's successor in command of the reconstituted Western Desert Force in April 1941 was Lieutenant-General Sir Noel Beresford-Peirse, who was in charge during operations *Brevity* and *Battleaxe*. Commissioned in 1907, Beresford-Peirse was the kind of career officer who was exactly the opposite of Rommel. The son of a colonel in the Indian Army, he attended the staff college in the mid-1920s and won his reputation under O'Connor as commander of the 4th Indian Division. The failure of *Battleaxe* would prove such a reputation exaggerated and Beresford-Peirse was made GOC in Sudan. At the same time the Commander-in-Chief Middle East, General Sir Archibald Percival Wavell, was relieved of command. General Sir Claude Auchinleck took his place on 5 July 1941 and a few months later started a major reorganization of the British forces in North Africa.

Having been in charge while the British and Commonwealth forces won victory after victory in the Mediterranean and in Africa, Wavell had become a kind of a legend. Under his command the Italians had been defeated in East Africa and in Cyrenaica; however, the defeats suffered in Greece and Crete at German hands, along with the failure of *Battleaxe*, would prove fatal for him. Rommel appreciated Britain's most-discussed commander bar Montgomery. In his words he was the only British officer 'who showed a touch of genius' (*The Rommel Papers*, p. 520), probably an acknowledgement of the decision to hold Tobruk, which so frustrated Rommel's own plans. With the formation of Eighth Army on 26 September 1941, British generalship in the Western Desert seems to have worsened. Auchinleck was commissioned in 1904 and served in the Middle East during World War I, attended staff college in the late 1920s and was sent to Norway in May 1940. Described as a man of 'fresh mind and a hitherto untaxed personal energy' by Churchill, he would eventually disappoint him in his command of what had by then turned into the major theatre of Britain's war effort. His first mistake was in his choice of commander of Eighth Army, General Sir Alan Gordon Cunningham (younger brother of the famous admiral), an artillery officer commissioned in 1906 who had distinguished himself in the campaign against the Italian East Africa earlier in the war. In spite of his acknowledgement as a master of mobile operations, Cunningham was described by Rommel, like his successor Ritchie, as not a tank specialist and 'therefore, unable to introduce any far-reaching modernisation into British training'. Also, both 'rarely managed to commit their forces correctly according to the tactical requirements of mobile warfare' (*The Rommel Papers*, p. 520). Auchinleck, on the other hand, was seen as a 'very good leader' who 'usually left control of tactical operations to his subordinate commanders, who soon allowed me to call the tune, and who reacted more frequently than they acted, often without real necessity' (*The Rommel Papers*, p. 520).

Operation *Crusader* of 1942 would show all the differences that existed between the German and the British forces. The former (thanks mainly to the *Auftragstaktik* concept) were used to tactical flexibility, speed and decisiveness, the latter suffered from a rigid command structure, further exacerbated, to use Rommel's words, by the fact that 'most senior British officers [had] a certain tendency to think along established lines' (*The Rommel Papers*, p. 520). Rommel's belated reaction to the start of *Crusader* might suggest he was, at least on this occasion, overwhelmed by those thinking 'along established lines', but it was in the crisis that followed the battle of the Sunday of the dead that would show the difference between the two approaches. While Rommel personally took the lead of the armoured bulk of Panzergruppe Afrika, driving it through the useless 'dash to the wire',

Cunningham had no clue about what was going on in the battle as he was located at his command post at Fort Maddalena, some 100km (60 miles) from Sidi Rezegh. He would learn of the setback only in the afternoon, after a visit to the HQ of Godwin-Austen's XIII Corps during which plans were laid to regroup Eighth Army for the final, victorious pursuit. Cunningham's reaction is revealing. He went to a meeting with Auchinleck with the simple aim of deciding whether the offensive should be called off, his likely choice, or not. In the end it was Auchinleck's decision to stand fast, indirectly supported by Rommel's mistake, that saved the day and the battle for the British. Auchinleck resolved on relieving Cunningham from command, replacing him on 25 November with the deputy chief of the general staff of Middle East Command, Lieutenant-General Sir Neil Ritchie, for the very simple reason he was already familiar with the *Crusader* plan.

Ritchie would prove Auchinleck's worst choice for, apart from *Crusader*, he led Eighth Army into the disaster that was Gazala and was eventually relieved by Auchinleck, who personally took command over Eighth Army. It would be a mistake to have this failure resting on Ritchie's shoulders alone, however, since it was the culmination of a woefully managed system. Since June 1940 British forces in the Western Desert had had four different field commanders (O'Connor, Beresford-Peirse, Cunningham and Ritchie) and two theatre commanders (Wavell and Auchinleck), the total count rising respectively to six and three by the time of El Alamein. This makes an average of one field commander every five months and one theatre commander every ten. For the sake of comparison, Rommel was in charge for some 20 months and the Afrikakorps had five commanders between February 1941 and November 1942, not including Bayerlein who was temporary commander twice. Between 1941 and 1942 the British Eighth Army also had 20 different divisions or equivalent under command, including Commonwealth, Dominion and Imperial. Only four of them (the 1st and 7th British Armoured Divisions, 4th Indian and 1st South African) would fight in more than two battles, while the German 21. (and its predecessor 5. leichte) and 15. Panzer-Divisionen fought in all the battles from February 1941 to November 1942. This made it very hard to put into practice experience acquired on the battlefield and further aggravated the problems of an army excessively tied to its pre-war doctrines and tactics. The highly centralized British command system, which was structured by the principles of top-down command, was governed by strict discipline and instant obedience. Orders were always written and detailed, designed to bind subordinate commanders to the operational plan. Personal initiative was certainly not encouraged and, above all, British commanders did not lead from the front – a consequence both of O'Connor's capture and the nature of their command system, which required constant safe communications with higher headquarters. Personal relationship at the highest level also worsened the situation. One of Auchinleck's faults was his constant interference with Eighth Army's commanders, first Cunningham and then Ritchie, which resulted in a loss of trust and confidence from their subordinates.

This scenario could not happen on the German side, for the command system encouraged personal initiative. When Crüwell decided to ignore Rommel's order he simply exercised a prerogative of his own, which did not lessen the authority of the superior commander. Rommel's almost monomaniacal adherence to the idea of leading from the front and his mistake in dashing to the wire certainly cost him the final victory in the winter battle of 1941, but the rigid British command system and the inadequacy of its high-level command during *Crusader* would prevent the destruction of the bulk of the Axis forces in North Africa and a complete victory, with the result that, two months after his decision to withdraw, Rommel was back at Gazala. The spring and summer of 1942 marked the lowest ebb of British command in North Africa; Ritchie, chosen as Eighth Army's commander for the simple reason he was on the spot, proved to be something of a disaster. Commissioned in 1914 in the Black Watch, during World War I he served in France and the Middle East; after attending staff courses in the late 1920s, he was in Palestine in 1937–38 and, at the outbreak of World War II, became chief of staff of Brooke's II Corps in France. In May 1941 he became deputy chief of general staff of MEC, until Auchinleck chose him for Eighth Army. Ritchie had some technical skills, and under his command some attempts were made to improve the flexibility and cooperation between infantry and tank formations, principally through the formation of the armoured brigade groups. On the other hand he had many shortcomings, not least in lack of experience of command of large formations and troublesome relationships with both his superior and his subordinates; Auchinleck kept him on a very short leash, while his corps commanders, Lieutenant-Generals Charles Willoughby Norrie and William Gott, were close friends and would club together practising 'a sort of joint command by confabulation' (Tim Moreman, *Desert Rats*, p. 56), which effectively shut him out of decision-making.

In May–June 1942 an experienced and determined Rommel confronted this feeble command structure with his well-trained Panzerarmee Afrika and the results were inevitable. Auchinleck's own command of the Eighth Army, after the removal of Ritchie on 25 June, would demonstrate the difference between a defeated and a beaten force: command. Rommel's own words fully acknowledge Auchinleck's accomplishments: 'Every time I was on the point of forcing a break-through with my German motorised formations, he launched an attack on the Italians elsewhere, scattered them and either penetrated uncomfortably close to our supply area or threatened a break-through in the south. On each occasion I was forced to break off my own attack in order to hurry to the help of the threatened sector' (*The Rommel Papers*, p. 520). Auchinleck was removed on 15 August, replaced as Commander-in-Chief Middle East by General Sir Harold Alexander and as commander of Eighth Army by Lieutenant-General Sir Bernard Law Montgomery, who eventually became Rommel's nemesis.

Like Rommel, Montgomery (commissioned in 1908) had no family military background, was an instructor at the Staff College in Camberley,

Field Marshal Sir Bernard Law Montgomery was Rommel's nemesis in both North Africa and Normandy. Though they were quite different personalities, and excelled in different styles of warfare, both possessed exceptional charisma and leadership capabilities. (Library of Congress)

served in France during World War I and, by 1940, was a commander who was both hard to work with and who appreciated publicity and the importance of modern media. The similarities ended here though, for in 1920 'Monty' attended staff college himself, which undoubtedly contributed to shaping his methodical, well-planned and thoroughly efficient command system, exactly the opposite of Rommel's 'bold decision' style of command. Monty left nothing to chance, he was not a field commander and avoided those 'bold decisions' that had made the name of his most famous enemy. In his own words, Rommel would be the first to introduce the argument used later by Correlli Barnett to criticize Montgomery, that he 'was in a position to profit by the bitter experience of his predecessor'.

> He did not leave the slightest detail out of his calculations. He discounted all academic theorising and let himself be guided by experience alone. He showed himself very advanced in his thinking when, on arriving at El Alamein, he worked out the essential rules of the front for himself and proceeded to shape his method of attack accordingly. His principle was to fight no battle unless he knew for certain that he would win it. Of course this is a method which will only work given material superiority; but that he had. He was cautious – to my mind, excessively so – but then he could afford to be.
> *The Rommel Papers*, p. 521

The reality is that Rommel and Montgomery were very different types of commanders. The former being accustomed to directing his forces on the battlefield, relying heavily on improvisation, while the latter (as Rommel himself pointed out) was much more of a strategist, best suited for well-planned and prepared battles. As such, the two never faced each other on even terms in either El Alamein or Normandy. Both battles were largely decided by the material superiority that Montgomery had been able to achieve. On both occasions Rommel was unable to wage that kind of warfare best suited to him, the mobile, fluctuating kind in which a timely decision could make all the difference.

WHEN WAR IS DONE

Erwin Rommel died on 14 October 1944 by committing suicide with cyanide, which was supplied him on Hitler's order along with a proposal: either take it or face a public trial for his involvement in the 20 July plot to assassinate the Führer. Today the common opinion is that Rommel was aware of the conspiracy, though to what extent it is hard to say, but not involved at all in the plot. The reason why Rommel chose suicide over trial is buried with him.

Rommel, the man and the commander, is somehow harder to understand than his myth. Without any doubt he was a very talented and skilled field commander, one who proved himself on the battlefield in a way that defines the term bravery. He was a gifted commander, with his ability to appreciate the situation and react swiftly, and he was also a very good leader whose soldiers followed and obeyed him. His achievements as a platoon and then battalion commander during World War I are remarkable and there is no question that this is what Rommel knew best, and what he really excelled in. As such Rommel perfectly fitted the German command system based on the concept of leading from the front, and the eventual development of the

Following his suicide on 14 October 1944, Rommel was buried four days later with a state ceremony in Ulm, which was attended by Generalfeldmarschall von Rundstedt. (HITM)

The 'Desert Fox' at war. How Rommel might have chosen to be remembered: on the battlefield, giving orders to his men. (HITM)

Stosstrupp tactics. There is no doubt at all that, should Rommel's career never have been fast-tracked at all, he would have been a first-class field unit commander at battalion and regimental level.

The point is that Rommel's career was fast-tracked, and all of a sudden he was propelled into a completely new dimension, which makes his achievements hard to evaluate. Rommel's experiences as a divisional commander during the campaign in the West in 1940 were just too short to provide a fair showcase of his skills in such a new role. Rommel was bold and brave in a way that was uncommon amongst German Panzer division commanders, he also proved himself innovative and more skilled than other commanders of much greater experience. Yet, a closer examination muddies the picture somewhat. During the crossing of the Meuse the neighbouring 5. Panzer-Division was to play a decisive role in support of Rommel's own 7. Panzer-Division, which is not always acknowledged. Perhaps most importantly, Rommel would have been the last to acknowledge the role of others on the battlefield and seemed at times to be playing the game alone. His own genuine capabilities as a field commander would be counterbalanced by an almost complete inability to be part of a broader battle plan. It was hard for Rommel to fit himself into someone else's plans, and he made no secret of it.

In a number of instances, Rommel found himself in tricky situations that arose directly

A hard, unfriendly environment like the Western Desert was hell for the soldier, but in the meantime it was heaven for the fast, mobile kind of warfare Rommel preferred. A PzKpfw IV tank on the move. (Carlo Pecchi)

from his own style of command. The troubles 7. Panzer-Division faced at Arras originated from his desire to advance further and faster than others. However, having created these problems his personal intervention on the battlefield also solved most of them.

Rommel's characteristic hallmark was that of leading from the front. It was not uncommon for German generals, even at army corps level, to be with the spearhead units to appreciate first hand the situation on the battlefield, but no one would ever match the level that Rommel achieved. Not only did he lead the spearheads, but he did it as an army commander which, even by German standards, was exceptional. That may not always work, but it certainly contributed to his wartime myth. However, once the North African campaign had finished and he was given other commands matching his rank, he would find himself in positions that did not really suit him. His unschooled and untrained talent and skills worked well in North Africa, but did not in Normandy where Rommel was a a round peg in a square hole.

Why exactly Rommel was chosen for North Africa is not entirely clear. In a way, his inability to cooperate amicably made his relationship with the Italians and German high command very difficult. On the other hand this might have been the very quality that made him the best choice for the job. A more cautious commander, someone concerned about cooperation and careful planning, might have achieved some victories, but would have been hard pressed to match Rommel's spectacular successes in the Western Desert. He certainly made mistakes, and lacked an overall strategic view of the campaign, but on the other hand his skills, toughness and will-power were

Rommel amongst his soldiers. Taking care of them was a duty for him, as he wrote in his *Papers*: 'It is sheer nonsense to say that maintenance of the men's morale is the job of the battalion commander alone. The higher the rank, the greater the effect of the example. The men tend to feel no kind of contact with a commander who, they know, is sitting somewhere in headquarters. What they want is what might be termed a physical contact with him' (p. 241). (HITM)

elements that made the difference during the campaign and brought the Axis close to victory. One could argue whether he could or should have won the campaign, but one thing is for sure: Rommel was the 'Desert Fox', the perfect commander for that kind of war.

INSIDE THE MIND

In many ways Rommel was a very simple man. The characteristics he displayed as a field commander give us a fairly simple outline of his character; he was courageous, strong-willed, determined, self-confident and extremely hard on himself. All these qualities enabled him to face the battlefield without hesitation, to appreciate a situation quickly and to react promptly, more often than not making bold decisions. As an officer, however, Rommel would discover that his social background was a serious hindrance to his military career. The events surrounding his award of the Pour le Mérite award reinforced the message that there would always be someone else who, because of their background, would have an easier route to the top than Rommel. The lesson Rommel seems to have learned was simple; if he wanted to be acknowledged for his achievements, he had to make sure there could be no mistake about them. If he was to stand out, then he must do so by winning stunning successes on the battlefield, proving his ability as a commander and leader. His was a struggle to achieve a position of greatness in the face of the disadvantages of his birth and the Prussian attitudes of the German Army of his day.

Rommel was without any doubt a very brave and skilled field commander, but also had an instinctive distrust of that 'academic stuff' that might have helped his career. There are some references in his papers to this attitude; the matter of overseas transport across the Mediterranean was '… the product of obsolete opinions and betrayed the tendency of the academic mind to evade all difficulties and prove them insurmountable.' What mattered was '… the power of execution, the ability to direct one's whole energies towards the fulfilment of a particular task'. And thus 'The officer of purely intellectual attainments is usually only fitted for work as an assistant on the staff; he can criticise and provide the material for discussion' (*The Rommel Papers*, p. 288). Also, in his comments on modern military leadership, written in 1944, Rommel criticized the intellectual attitude of the Reichswehr in which '… officers came to be assessed on their intellectual qualification alone'. It was such an attitude that led the European general staffs to '… unquestioningly accepting the views of great men in matters of principle,' thus getting themselves '… lost in the detail, tangled it all up into a dreadful complexity, turned warfare into an exchange of memoranda and stuck to their ideas through thick and thin' (*The Rommel Papers*, p. 516).

The Germans were not exempt from these attitudes, with even the German officer corps being '… by no means completely free of the old

Rommel at the end of a reconnaissance flight aboard a Fieseler Fi 156 Stork; Rommel's skill and capabilities as a field commander were not matched by his strategic vision. (HITM)

prejudices' and 'stuck to their established methods and precedents, even though these often showed themselves to be outdated and hence false'. On the other hand 'My staff and I gave no regard whatever to all this unnecessary academic nonsense, which had long been overtaken by technical development. Consequently, many officers of the academic type, steeped in their ancient theories, failed to understand us and so took us for adventurers, amateurs and the like' (*The Rommel Papers*, p. 517).

These attitudes show Rommel clearly as a stubborn man, single-minded and strictly bound to the security of what was familiar to him. What Rommel knew best was leading his troops into battle and, apart from a degree of interest in technical details, he shied away from any of those 'intellectual attitudes' that did not interest him.

Although this did not necessarily lessen his capabilities as a field commander, it certainly made him difficult to deal with, both for his superiors and his subordinates. He would rarely take another's advice, or even orders, and was always ready to blame others for any failure rather than to seek out for the real causes.

An open-minded attitude towards 'intellectual stuff' might have made a difference in Rommel's decision-making. His was a straightforward process – success on the battlefield almost inevitably led him to see a grand victory within his grasp, and he would reach for it. A tactical or operational victory would simply not suffice, especially in North Africa. The only goal he could see was the strategic victory at the Suez Canal, the only one great enough for him.

Rommel was surely ambitious in his career and also vain to a certain extent, as the many photographs of him testify. Yet it would be wrong to see him as a mere publicity seeker. Actions such as sending Hitler a narrative of the 7. Panzer-Division's achievements in the 1940 campaign were a consequence of the events related to the award of the Pour le Mérite. His keen attitude towards the media, also suggest an uncommon understanding of modern communications. Rommel was not just eager to be in the pictures, he was also a photographer himself and used the media as a tool to draw attention to himself and his troops who otherwise might have been forgotten. Thanks to his actions, practically everybody knew (and knows today) about the Afrikakorps and the war in North Africa, something other units elsewhere failed to achieve.

There was also more to Rommel than just meets the eye in his attitude towards Hitler and the Nazi party. Even though Goebbels would see him as 'one of us', Rommel's keen attitude was probably influenced by the fact that it was thanks to Hitler and the Nazis that his career had a second start, and that

Rommel talking to a member of his staff seated inside 'Mammut', a captured British command vehicle that Rommel used extensively during the first part of the North African campaign. (HITM)

he had victories to win. This attitude was in turn influenced by the turn of military events. The Rommel of 1943–44 was disillusioned, pessimistic about the war and its outcome. Certainly he saw the defence of north-west Europe against the invasion as the last chance, both for Germany and his own career, and when he realized the battle for Normandy was lost he simply blamed the only person he could still blame: Hitler. Rommel knew of the conspiracy against him, but not of the bomb attack of 20 July 1944. One can easily see the appeal of the plot to him, there is no glory for defeated commanders and seeking for an alternative to Hitler was the only way to negotiate a peace with the Allies, which he might have done himself. This was probably the only chance he could see to give his career a new start, and avoid the mediocrity of defeat.

A LIFE IN WORDS

Rommel was already some kind of a myth in his lifetime after his successes in the war in North Africa brought him fame and acknowledgements far beyond the boundaries of Germany. It was as much the importance attributed to him by his enemies that eventually created the Rommel myth. There was one simple explanation why the British forces in North Africa, who in early 1941 seemed on the point of winning the campaign, faced another year and a half of war in that theatre, often with some serious setbacks and the threat of defeat: Rommel. He was the key to everything, at least for the average soldier as well as for the audience at home, and only one thing mattered: to defeat him. A perfect example of how popular a figure Rommel was, even amongst his enemies, is illustrated by the fact that he was the only German general to be portrayed, as a main character, in a feature film entitled *Five Graves to Cairo* released in 1943 by the director Billy Wilder for Paramount. Erich von Stroheim's characterization of the 'Desert Fox,' a much more popular sobriquet amongst the British than the Germans, may have been far from the reality, but it certainly contributed to give rise to Rommel's myth.

Throughout 1943 and 1944, Rommel was no longer the centre of attention for audiences in enemy countries for the very simple reason that he had been defeated and ultimate victory for the Allies seemed not only certain, but close at hand. When, less than seven months after his death, the war in Europe was over and Hitler's Third Reich defeated, Rommel was more a shadow of the past than the myth he once had been. However, it took only a few years before the myth would start a life anew, largely due to the circumstances surrounding Rommel's death.

To put the story in its context, one ought to remember a very simple fact: in 1945 Germany was a defeated country, in a much poorer condition than in 1918. This time she and her armed forces were not just facing defeat, but were also blamed for the Nazi wars of aggression and for the war crimes that had been committed. From this point of view Rommel was the perfect general; he had been some kind of a hero not only for the Germans, but for Germany's enemies as well. He had never fought in the gruesome cauldron of the Eastern Front, in the ideological war between Nazism and Communism. Rather he always fought against the Western Allies, better still he fought in the only theatre of war – North Africa – where, either because of environmental conditions or of the lack of any ideology, nothing was experienced that could be remotely compared to the brutal conditions of warfare on the Eastern Front. Last but not least, Rommel was portrayed effectively as one of those who opposed Hitler and who died because of their involvement in the 20 July plot.

As early as September 1945 Rommel's family pointed out how the death of the *Generalfeldmarschall* had not been a consequence of the wounds inflicted by the air attack of 17 July 1944 in Normandy. A couple of years later it was Rommel's chief of staff in Normandy, General Hans Speidel (himself involved in the July plot), who set himself the task of making Rommel a 'national hero of the German people'. Such a task would lead to the publication in late 1949 of Speidel's memoirs entitled *Invasion 1944. Ein Beitrag zu Rommel und des Reiches Schicksal* (*A Contribution on Rommel and the Destiny of the Reich*) which portrayed him not only as a military leader but also, much more importantly, as one of the leading personalities of the German resistance against Hitler. The purpose of all this was clearly to show how the German Army had been made up not only of fanatical soldiers ready to fight for their Führer in the wars of aggression and extermination, but also of men whose hands were clean of any misdemeanour. Some of them, including leading personalities like Rommel, would eventually choose to fight the Nazi regime. Speidel would later become commander-in-chief of the new German Army, the Bundeswehr, in much the same way as Admiral Friedrich Ruge (Rommel's naval liaison in Normandy) became commander-in-chief of the new navy.

However, a large part of the Rommel myth was created with the help of his former enemies. It is unsurprising that Rommel's first biography was written in English by a Briton, Desmond Young, whose *Rommel* was first published in London in 1950, and many others have followed over the years. (It is worth noting Rommel is one of the very few German generals, certainly the most popular one, whose biographies have been written in English.) In 1951 a new feature film by Henry Hathaway was released by 20th Century Fox, based on Young's biography, *The Desert Fox* starring James Mason, who portrayed Rommel in a much more sympathetic way than he had been shown eight years previously. Rommel was seen as loyal soldier with outstanding military and humane qualities, and a firm adversary of Hitler's politics. On a more professional basis, the British military theoretician and historian Basil Liddell Hart would largely contribute not only to Rommel's own myth but, following the example of Speidel, also to use it for the restoration of the moral authority of the German officers corps. Liddell Hart's book *The Other Side of the Hill: Germany's Generals, their Rise and Fall* (first published in 1948), as well as the introductory notes he wrote for the English edition of *The Rommel Papers* (first published in 1953), and the memoirs of Guderian and Manstein too, drew a neat distinction between the political goals of Hitler's Third Reich and the professional war-making German generals that still survives more or less intact. Given this start Rommel's myth developed a life of its own, which bore little resemblance to the wartime one and even to the one created on purpose shortly after the war

A cheerful Rommel, sporting the freshly awarded oak leaves and swords to his Knight's Cross, is driven inside Hitler's headquarters at Rastenburg in spring 1942. (NARA)

ended. Biographies and books dealing with the war in North Africa, all too often with the name of Rommel in their titles, had (and still have) large commercial success. Amongst these must be included the first attempt to re-assess Rommel's myth, his life and his military skills. David Irving's biography *Rommel: The Trail of the Fox*, published in 1977, posed Major questions about Rommel's character, his achievements as a military commander and the extent of his actual involvement in the anti-Hitler plot. None of this lessened his myth, rather it contributed to keeping it alive.

Yet, not even Rommel's myth would survive the greatest enemy of all: the passing of time. Following the downfall of the Soviet Union and of the Communist regimes in Eastern Europe, many of the political needs that gave rise to Rommel's post-war myth failed all of a sudden. Politicians and historians stepped back to the mood prevailing in the immediate aftermath of World War II. Nazism started to be seen as pure evil, and the German military as close associates sharing its crimes and guilt. Following the same pattern, Rommel's myth started to be denuded and honours granted to him were now seen as an embarrassing encumbrance. In 1961 a plaque in his honour was unveiled in the former officers' mess at Goslar, and the inspector general of the German Army greeted Rommel as 'the most magnificent soldier' and 'a role model for young soldiers.' Forty years later, in 2001, the plaque was removed with a very simple explanation: Rommel was associated with a criminal regime and as such represented it, therefore honouring him was to honour that regime. One may wonder what Rommel would have thought of all this? His myth has proved to be an enduring one and, in one way or another, he still is the focus of public attention. This is probably what Rommel might have wanted after all. Times and fashions will pass and change, but one can be sure that his name will always recur.

FURTHER READING

Although now largely outdated, Desmond Young's first biography *Rommel: The Desert Fox* (London, 1950) is still a perfectly readable and enjoyable account. Other biographies produced since the 60s have added little to it; amongst these are worth mentioning Ronald Lewin's *Rommel as Military Commander* (London, 1968) and Kenneth Macksey's *Rommel: Battles and Campaigns* (New York, 1979). The first detailed, and historically researched account of Rommel's life and military career is David Irving's *Rommel: The Trail of the Fox* (London, 1977), which provided the core of other biographies to follow. Richard D. Law and Craig Luther's *Rommel: A Narrative and Pictorial History* (San Jose, California, 1980) is more important for its photographic content, like Christer Jorgensen's *Rommel's Panzers: Rommel, Blitzkrieg and the Triumph of the Panzer Arm* (Staplehurst, 2003) and Karl Hoffman's *Erwin Rommel* (Commander in Focus; London, 2004).

More recently, several Rommel biographies have been produced taking into account both his life and career and the relevant issue of his myth; outstanding is David Fraser's *Knight's Cross: A Life of Field Marshal Erwin Rommel* (London, 1993). After a long interval, Rommel's first German biography was released in 1950 by Lutz Koch, *Erwin Rommel. Die Wandlung eines grossen Soldaten* (Stuttgart, 1950). More recently new biographies have been released in Germany as well. These are Ralf Georg Reuth's *Rommel. Des Führers General* (Munich, 1987), Maurice Philip Remy's *Mythos Rommel* (Berlin, 2002) and Ralf Georg Reuth's *Rommel: Das Ende einer Legende* (Munich, 2004), the latter also translated into English. Rommel is of course included in several books dealing with German generalship during the Second World War; worth mentioning is Corelli Barnett's edited title *Hitler's Generals* (London, 1989), with an essay by Martin Blumenson. Recently Rommel's personal history has been put in parallel with those of other famous generals; Dennis Showalter's *Patton and Rommel: Men of War in the Twentieth Century* (New York, 2005), and Terry Brighton's *Masters of Battle: Monty, Patton and Rommel at War* (London, 2008) definitely sanctioned Rommel's place in the history of great commanders.

Rommel's own work include his *Infanterie Greift an* (English reprint: London, 1990), the volume *Krieg ohne Hass* (*War Without Hate*) edited by his wife and Fritz Bayerlein (Brenz, 1950). Translated into English with additional material, mostly Rommel's letters to his wife, it was edited by Basil H. Liddell Hart, Lucie Marie Rommel, Manfred Rommel and Fritz Bayerlein as *The Rommel Papers* (London, 1953). Recently selected parts have been reprinted, edited by John Pimlott as *Rommel and His Art of War* (London, 2003).

A list of books dealing with Rommel, the Afrikakorps, the war in North Africa and in Normandy (just to mention some selected events in his life) would probably take more space than this entire work; worth mentioning are the works by Hans Otto Behrendt *Rommel's Intelligence in the Desert Campaign, 1941–1943* (London, 1985) and Friedrich Ruge *Rommel in Normandy: Reminiscences* (San Rafale, California, 1979). For British commanders in North Africa suggested reading includes Nick Smart's *British Generals of the Second World War* (Barnsley, 2005), W. G. F. Jackson's *The Battle for North Africa 1940–43* (New York, 1975), and David French's *Raising Churchill's Army: The British Army and the War against Germany 1919–1945* (Oxford, 2000). Nigel Hamilton's monumental three-volume biography of *Montgomery* (London, 1981–1986) is the best on the subject.

INDEX

References to illustrations are shown in **bold**. Plates are prefixed pl, with captions on the page in brackets.